THE SINATRA
SCRAPBOOK

THE SINATRA SCRAPBOOK

by GARY L. DOCTOR

A Citadel Press Book

PUBLISHED BY CAROL PUBLISHING GROUP

Copyright © 1991 by Gary L. Doctor

A Citadel Press Book
Published by Carol Publishing Group

Editorial Offices   Sales & Distribution Offices
600 Madison Avenue   120 Enterprise Avenue
New York, NY 10022   Secaucus, NJ 07094

In Canada: Musson Book Company
A Division of General Publishing Co., Limited
Don Mills, Ontario

Citadel Press is a registered trademark of
Carol Communications, Inc.

Queries regarding rights and permissions
should be addressed to: Carol Publishing Group,
600 Madison Avenue, New York, NY 10022

Manufactured in the United States of America
ISBN 0-8065-1250-4

10   9   8   7   6   5   4   3   2

Carol Publishing Group books are available at special discounts
for bulk purchases, for sales promotions, fund raising, or
educational purposes. Special editions can also be created to
specifications. For details contact: Special Sales Department,
Carol Publishing Group, 120 Enterprise Ave., Secaucus, NJ 07094

Library of Congress Cataloging-in-Publication Data

Doctor, Gary L.
     The Sinatra scrapbook/ by Gary L. Doctor
        p. cm.
        "A Citadel Press book."
        1. Sinatra, Frank, 1915- . 2. Singers--United States--
Biography. I. Title.
ML420.S565D6   1991
        782.42164'092--dc20
            [B]   91-28731
                                                            CIP
                                                            MN

TO MY WIFE MARY,
for her understanding, support, and love.

Acknowledgments

I thank my mother for taking me to my first Sinatra film and buying my first Sinatra record. My family's encouragement through the years is fondly appreciated.

My son Dustin took most of the photos, corrected my grammar, proofread, and typed. This book could not have been completed without him.

My collection is a result of years of deals and trades with other Sinatra enthusiasts around the world, and I thank these collectors for their help, cooperation, and friendship.

My friend Richard Apt contributed his knowledge and a few items from his extensive collection.

Among the many International Sinatra Society members who contributed items and information, my sincere appreciation goes to: Mr. & Mrs. J. P. Cerra, Phil Dalia, Mark Doctor, Joe Glovacz, Ed Jubb, Milton Sommers.

Thanks also to: ABC, Artanis Foods, Capitol Records, CBS Television, Columbia Pictures, Columbia Records, MCA, Metro-Goldwyn-Mayer, NBC, Paramount Pictures, RCA, Reprise Records, RKO, Turner Home Entertainment, *TV Guide*, 20th Century Fox, United Artists, Universal, Warner Bros. Pictures, Warner Bros. Records, and Warner Home Video.

Thank you, Mr. Sinatra, for filling my life with your music.

Contents

THE SINATRA
SCRAPBOOK

To Gary
all good wishes
Frank Sinatra

Introduction

Had he only been a radio personality, he would be known for hosting a dozen different series and countless guest appearances.

Had he only been a television celebrity, he would be known for numerous guest appearances, two series, and a group of specials in the 1960s including the Emmy-winning *A Man and His Music* in 1965.

Had he only been a star of the movies, he would be known for leading roles in more than fifty films plus several cameo appearances. He won a special Academy Award for *The House I Live In*, the 1945 short subject on tolerance, an Oscar for best supporting actor as Maggio in 1953's *From Here to Eternity*, and a best actor nomination for his portrayal of a drug addict in *The Man With the Golden Arm* in 1955.

Had he only sung live, he would be known as a nightclub headliner. He has appeared in Las Vegas from its beginning to the present and played most of the major saloons, showrooms, auditoriums, arenas, and coliseums around the world, thrilling millions who have seen him in concert.

Had he only been a recording artist, there would be almost two thousand songs in his repertoire. Dozens of his recordings topped the pop charts from the 1940s through the 1980s. He has won Grammys and had best-selling albums going gold and platinum in sales.

But Frank Sinatra has been ALL of these!

Those who seek Sinatra collectibles as a hobby find it rewarding because there is so much available. His career spans the late 1930s not to only today but into the future—as there will be new Sinatra items for years to come. A study of Frank Sinatra is a study of modern show business—a study in *Entertainment*.

Sinatra's fame is greatly due to hard work. Never one to rest on past achievements, Sinatra has always been extremely productive, often being busy by day, filming at the studio and filling evenings with nightclub or concert engagements. Early morning recording sessions often brought memorable results. A full career has produced a wealth of collectibles for his fans and followers.

One sheet (27 × 41 inch movie poster) for *Major Bowes' Amateur Theatre of the Air* does not picture Sinatra, but collectors wonder if there's another in the series with Frank.

Although his name does not appear, Sinatra sings parody of "High Hopes" on this presidential campaign record for JFK.

Major Bowes, center, with "The Hoboken Four" in 1935. From left, Frank Tamburro, Jimmy Petro, Patty Prince, and nineteen-year-old Frankie.

1. On Collecting

The wise collector will proceed under the premise that no one can have everything. A different philosophy not only will damage a collector's finances, but also frustrate the collector. Pursuing collectibles should be an enjoyable hobby, not a mania. In my dealings with other collectors, I'm sometimes asked to send the package to a work address—so the spouse "won't find out" another purchase has been made.

While it's always rewarding to add another treasure to one's collection, it's sweeter to find that rare gem at a flea market or garage sale for a fraction of the price a knowledgeable dealer will charge. I recall finding at a flea market the "High Hopes" record for John Kennedy's campaign among a stack of records marked "25¢ each." However, not everyone has the time to search for these hidden treasures and must rely on dealers as the major source of wanted items.

Collecting can be expensive, and money plays a factor in separating the man's collection from the boy's. However, having the funds is not as important as the opportunity to obtain the item. Having $200 to spend is often easier than finding that $200 item needed.

What makes collecting Sinatra so interesting is the prolificacy of his career. He did so much, in so many fields of entertainment, that no individual can hope to acquire all the memorabilia. Most serious collectors can claim something a fellow collector cannot. The vast variety holds our interest, and we delight in showing something the other guy doesn't have. The purpose of this book is not to show everything that's collectible on Sinatra, but to give an overall view of his amazing career, through the memorabilia of his work. Along the way, I hope even the most avid collector will find some unusual, not-seen-before items.

2. Major Bowes

(1935)

For our purpose of collecting Sinatra memorabilia, we date the beginning of his career to September 8, 1935, with an appearance on the *Major Bowes Amateur Hour*, a popular radio show of the day on which hopeful talents competed. With three other boys from his hometown, Sinatra appeared. They were The Hoboken Four, a singing quartet. What came out of this was the very first recording of the Sinatra voice discovered to date. Prior to their launching into a fine, snappy rendition of "Shine," a nineteen-year-old, filled with confidence, declared, "I'm Frank . . . Major. We're looking for jobs. How about it?

Everyone that's ever heard us, liked us. We think we're pretty good!"

The Hoboken Four made a second appearance on Bowes's radio show and, although they never won the amateur contest, they were given a job touring with an "amateur" company. In a series of movie shorts titled *Major Bowes' Amateur Theatre of the Air* emerged what would be the first of Sinatra on film. However, no print is known to exist. The film's director, John Auer, claims that the boys looked so lean, he put them in blackface for a minstrel show.

3. Harry James

(1939)

Sinatra often shares a thought or memory with his audience as he comments during a performance. More than once he's said something from the stage that led to a "situation" or alienated an entire country. Occasionally a fond remembrance is expressed. Reflecting on his days before meeting Harry James:

"I had a nice job in the Rustic Cabin. I got about fifteen clams a week. I used to sweep the floors, sing the songs, show the people to the tables, and bow to the boss."

Not doing much better than Sinatra in 1939, but hearing Frankie at Englewood, New Jersey's Rustic Cabin, Harry James offered him the male vocalist position with the newly formed James band. In addition to a weekly salary of $75 and a two-year contract, this would give Sinatra the exposure he needed. Not only was the 1939 World's Fair in the New York City area, but the James band played the Roseland Ballroom in midtown Manhattan most of that summer.

In a New York recording studio, July 13, 1939, Sinatra makes his first commercial record, "From the Bottom of My Heart," backed with "Melancholy Mood," on the Brunswick label. This 78 rpm record did not receive a celebrated release. Neither song made the pop charts. Neither is memorable. Yet, Brunswick 8443 is the most valued record among Sinatra collectors because it is the first. This is where that vast, wonderful library of his records begins, and his only one on the Brunswick label. If you have a Brunswick 78 rpm record with Sinatra's name on it, you have THE record.

Sinatra recorded ten songs with Harry James by November 8. Four years later, one of those recordings, "All or Nothing at All," would reach the Number Two position on *Billboard*'s chart.

The very first Frank Sinatra record. Note the phrase "Vocal Chorus Frank Sinatra" to the right of the center hole. Brunswick 8443 was recorded July 13, 1939, in New York City.

British issue of Sinatra's first recording.

"From the Bottom of My Heart" pressing from Chile reads "Canta: Frank Sinatra."

"All or Nothing at All" became a big hit four years after it was recorded. Here's the song sheet.

The ten songs Sinatra recorded with Harry James in 1939 have been available on a variety of records over the years. All are on this LP/CD from the Sinatra Music Society, England.

4. **Tommy Dorsey**

(1940–1942)

Sinatra's stint as male vocalist with the Tommy Dorsey band brought eighty-three recorded sides and appearances in two feature films. These songs, recorded 1940 through 1942, were hard to acquire in later years as they were also sought by collectors of Bunny Berigan, Buddy Rich, Joe Bushkin, Ziggy Elman, and other Dorsey band members, as well as "The Sentimental Gentleman" himself. Adding to the difficulty of acquiring these eighty-three historic tracks, one side of a Dorsey 78 rpm may feature Sinatra, but the flip side may be an instrumental or a vocal by Jo Stafford or the Pied Pipers.

RCA Limited in England reissued all of the Dorsey and Sinatra collaborations with its 1972 release of *The Dorsey/Sinatra Sessions 1940–1942* (SD-1000), a six-record box set. RCA in the States reissued the entire Dorsey/Sinatra library in 1982 in the form of three separate two-record sets.

With Dorsey, Sinatra scored on the pop charts for the first time. "All or Nothing at All," recorded with Harry James in 1939, didn't hit the charts until 1942. "I'll Never Smile Again" reached *Billboard*'s Number One position in 1940. Other classic Dorsey/Sinatra titles included "Imagination," "Stardust," "Oh, Look at Me Now," "Everything Happens to Me," "This Love of Mine," "Daybreak," "There Are Such Things," "It Started All Over Again," and "It's Always You." Twenty Sinatra recordings made *Billboard*'s Top Ten between 1940 and 1942, and he continued to have his recordings on *Billboard*'s charts into 1980 with "New York, New York."

Song sheet from *Las Vegas Nights*. Sinatra is in top row, far right.

Original one sheet poster.

Song sheet from *Ship Ahoy*.

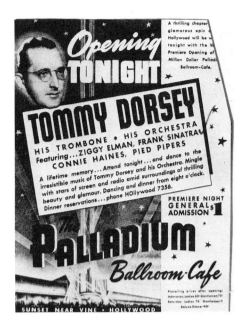

A young "Blue Eyes" made his feature film debut as a member of Dorsey's group and in 1941 sang "I'll Never Smile Again" in Paramount Pictures' *Las Vegas Nights*. A year later, again with the Dorsey band, he sang "The Last Call for Love," "Poor You," and "Moonlight Bay" (as Eleanor Powell tap-dances a Morse code message) in MGM's *Ship Ahoy*.

When big bands were at their height of popularity, the Tommy Dorsey aggregation was at the top of the heap, king of the hill. In addition to films and records, Dorsey was often heard on radio via live remote. Home listeners enjoyed Sinatra in broadcasts from Frank Dailey's Meadowbrook in Cedar Grove, New Jersey, or the Palladium Ballroom Cafe on Sunset Boulevard in Hollywood, or the Capitol Theatre in Washington, D.C. Beyond the records, radio, and films, Sinatra has credited his breath control and phrasing to Dorsey.

When he said good-bye to Tommy on September 3, 1942 (this farewell can be heard on RCA's *The Tommy Dorsey/Frank Sinatra Radio Years*). Frank's name was a household word.

Ten-inch 78 rpm record.

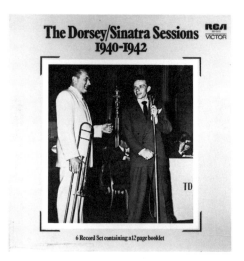

Box set of all the Dorsey/ Sinatra recordings was issued in England, 1972.

Ten-inch LP.

A ten-inch 78 rpm record was pressed to promote *The Dorsey/ Sinatra Sessions* issued by RCA in 1982. Number one was presented to then President Ronald Reagan; number thirty-one is pictured here.

From left, Frankie, Red Skelton, Eleanor Powell, Tommy Dorsey, Virginia O'Brien, and Bert Lahr in *Ship Ahoy*.

Poster promoting RCA's 1982 release of *The Dorsey/Sinatra Sessions 1940–1942.*

Song sheets from the Dorsey days.

Shortly after its release in the 1950's, *Frankie and Tommy* was withdrawn and replaced with a less conspicuous Sinatra on the cover and in the title. Both are RCA LPM-1569.

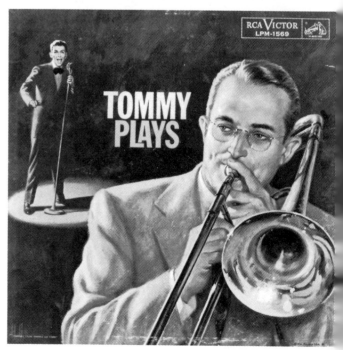

YOUNG FRANK SINATRA

Two LP set from Japan contains Dorsey/Sinatra tracks.

Frankie, top row far right.

5. Reveille With Beverly

(1943)

The August 15, 1942, *Down Beat* announces that Sinatra will soon leave the Dorsey band and has signed with General Amusement Corporation (GAC), third-ranking talent agency behind Music Corporation of America (MCA) and William Morris. "Good-bye, Tommy," then Frankie goes to Hollywood for his first billed film appearance, in Columbia Pictures' *Reveille With Beverly*.

Dressed in black tails, surrounded by pretty girls, Sinatra sings Cole Porter's "Night and Day." His three minute appearance is only one in a variety of acts including Bob Crosby, Duke Ellington, Count Basie, and the Mills Brothers.

23

Ad from *Billboard Band Yearbook*,
September 26, 1942.

By the time the film is released, Sinatra will be billed as the star.

While in Hollywood, Frank had hoped to secure the position of staff singer at NBC. When this attempt failed, he returned East to appear on CBS radio's *Coast to Coast*.

Original one-sheet poster.

6. **On His Own**

With filming on *Reveille With Beverly* completed, Frankie did his first New York stage performance sans the Dorsey band. Booked as an "extra added attraction" for the New Year's show at the Paramount on Broadway, he would stay on four additional weeks. The program read "The Voice That Has Thrilled Millions," but headliner Benny Goodman, not knowing a thing about this young performer, introduced him with a simple: "And now, Frank Sinatra."

The huge roar from the audience that erupted so surprised Benny, he is quoted to have asked "What the ---- was that?"

THE WEDGWOOD ROOM

At Supper FRANK SINATRA • Dinner and Supper EMIL COLEMAN and his Orchestra MISCHA BORR and his Orchestra alternating at Supper • Cover from 10:30, $2 • SUNDAY DINNER-DANCE...Mischa Borr and his Orchestra (no cover)

THE WALDORF-ASTORIA

Park Avenue at 50th Street

October 1, 1943, opening in New York attracts Park Avenue set.

Sinatra placed this ad in *Metronome* for Christmas 1942.

SWOONER-CROONER

Satellites sigh and scream as Singing
Sensation Sinatra solos with symphony

The road to respectability among adults included concerts with New York Philharmonic on August 3, 1943, and west for August 14 date with Los Angeles Philharmonic, fund-raisers for both orchestras.

Sinatra is billed as "The Voice That Has Thrilled Millions" on this program from opening at the Paramount.

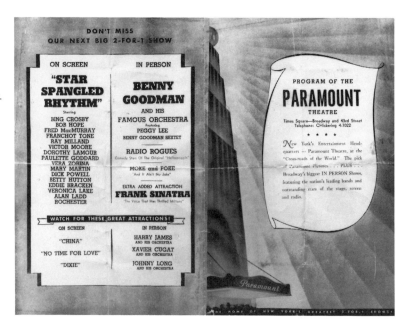

First "live" performance without Dorsey is at New York's Paramount for a December 30, 1942, opening.

7. The Radio Years

The Major Bowes appearance September 8, 1935, gave audio collectors the first recording of "The Voice." On April 18, 1988, the Mutual Broadcasting System presented "Come Swing with Me—Frank Sinatra in Concert," a ninety-minute stereo concert performance of "The Chairman" in fine form. The nearly fifty-three years between these two airings offered hundreds of hours of Sinatra programming.

Video systems vary from country to country, making video tapes in the U.S., for instance, incompatible with those in Great Britain. Audio discs and tapes, on the other hand, have always been compatible, and buffs around the world could easily exchange material. Some of the author's longest lasting relationships with other collectors began with an exchange of Sinatra on reel-to-reel tape (before the popularity of the audio cassette). Many forties radio shows were transcribed onto discs for the Armed Forces Radio Services, and it is not unusual for a "new discovery" (old radio show) to surface in Italy or Australia.

Shows intended to be aired once have survived the years and continue to entertain today's audio tape enthusiasts. As in the other areas of entertainment, Sinatra produced much in radio.

During the struggling years, following the Major Bowes tour and prior to Frank's signing with Harry James, local radio was a staple for a young Sinatra seeking only to be heard. Dinah Shore shared a WNEW microphone with Frank in New York City at this time. Well aware of the importance of exposure, he sought to perform in clubs that were wired for remote radio broadcasts. Tommy Dorsey and his band played such places, and we have hours of Sinatra on tape. The radio broadcasts give us variations of songs he recorded. More rewarding, we often get to hear Sinatra perform a song on radio that he never recorded. For the likes of "Too Fat Polka,"

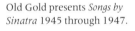
Old Gold presents *Songs by Sinatra* 1945 through 1947.

"The Woody Woodpecker Song," "The Dicky Bird Song," "Feudin' and Fightin'," "Tenderly," "S'Wonderful," or "Ave Maria," we have the radio shows.

Sinatra's farewell to the Dorsey band was broadcast September 3, 1942. A month later, beginning the week of October 4, Frank was heard twice weekly on CBS Radio's *Coast to Coast*. This was a sustaining program, paid for by the network rather than by a commercial sponsor. The February 1943 *Metronome* announced Sinatra's signing to do *Your Hit Parade*.

The shows he hosted, the guests appearing on his shows, the shows on which he was the guest, the songs he sang, the celebrities with whom he appeared, the dates, the details, could fill volumes. The radiography of his regular series suggests the scope of his work in this media. These old shows surface on occasion, keeping the audio collector active in today's world of music video.

"Command Performance" musical adaptation of Dick Tracy was broadcast April 29, 1945, and later appeared on these LPs.

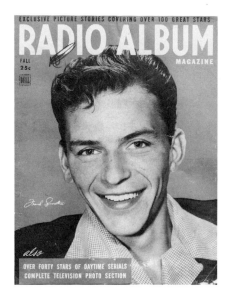 Magazines.

RADIOGRAPHY

(chronicling regular series Sinatra had on radio.)

Coast to Coast	CBS	Twice weekly beginning week of October 4, 1942
Your Hit Parade	CBS	Saturdays 9:00pm, February 27, 1943–December 30, 1944
Broadway Bandbox	CBS	Fridays May 14, 1943 11:15pm–12:00am Mondays July 19, 1943 9:30–10:00pm Sundays September 19, 1943–October 17, 1943
Songs by Sinatra	CBS	Sundays October 24, 1943–November 1943
Frank Sinatra Program (Vimms Vitamins)	CBS	Sundays November 14, 1943–June 14, 1944
Frank Sinatra in Person (Vimms Vitamins)	CBS	August 16, 1944–December 25, 1944
The Frank Sinatra Show (Max Factor)	CBS	January 3, 1945–May 23, 1945
Songs by Sinatra (Old Gold)	CBS	September 12, 1945–June 5, 1946
	CBS	September 18, 1946–June 4, 1947
Your Hit Parade (Lucky Strike)	NBC	September 6, 1947–May 28, 1949
Light Up Time (Lucky Strike)	NBC	Weekdays, September 5, 1949–May 1, 1950 3:00–3:15pm, repeated 8:00–8:15pm
Meet Frank Sinatra (Tinthair)	CBS	November 12, 1950–January 1951
Rocky Fortune	NBC	October 6, 1953–March 16, 1954
To Be Perfectly Frank	NBC	Tuesday and Friday, November 27, 1953–April 1955 8:15–8:30pm
The Bobbi Show	NBC	Wednesday and Friday, December 22, 1954–May 25, 1955

August 16, 1944 with Fredric March

August 23, 1944 with Rise Stevens

August 30, 1944 with Joan Leslie

September 6, 1944 with Orson Welles

September 20, 1944 with Joan Blondell

September 27, 1944 with Oscar Levant

October 25, 1944 with Milton Berle

Ads for the Vimms Vitamins series, depicting Sinatra with some of his guests.

Discs with public service announcements for radio stations.

8. Columbia Records

(1943–1952)

For a singing sensation on the rise, the wartime forties were not a good time to pursue a recording career. In a contract dispute, James Petrillo, then head of the American Federation of Musicians, called for a musicians' ban on recording. Live performances, including those on radio, were permitted but musicians were not to take part in recording sessions.

Record companies searched their vaults to reissue discs made prior to the ban, and Mannie Sachs, Artists and Repertoire head at Columbia, decided to put out again the 1939 "All or Nothing at All" by Frank with Harry James. This time around, the focus was on the vocal by Frank, and by summer of 1943, the record reached Number Two on the *Billboard* charts. Sinatra signed a two-year contract with Columbia effective June 1, 1943, but it was amended to November 11, 1944, once the Petrillo ban was lifted.

Ad for Columbia set issued in 1986.

Sinatra did record during the ban, a cappella, backed only by the Bobby Tucker Singers. There were nine songs by Frank without any instrumental accompaniment. "You'll Never Know," coupled with "Close to You," both recorded June 7, 1943, reached *Billboard*'s Number Two spot by July 22. "Sunday, Monday or Always" and "If You Please" (both recorded June 22) broke into the Top Ten by early September. Later

that month, "People Will Say We're in Love" backed with "Oh, What a Beautiful Morning!" (two tunes from that year's huge Broadway success *Oklahoma!*), recorded August 5, reached the Number Six position on the chart. "I Couldn't Sleep a Wink Last Night," coupled with "A Lovely Way to Spend an Evening," both recorded in November, reached the Number Five position by February 3, 1944. (The ninth side, "The Music Stopped," was initially released nearly twenty years later on the LP, *Sinatra in Hollywood*.)

What better way could Sinatra prove that his recording success need not rely on the Tommy Dorsey backings than by reaching the spots on the charts a cappella? It would be more than a year before Sinatra returned to the Columbia studio, November 14, 1944, after the lifting of the AFM recording ban.

"Why Try to Change Me Now?" was Frank's final session for Columbia on September 17, 1952, and then he was without a recording contract. Some of the hits Frank had on that red and gold Columbia label include: "Saturday Night Is the Loneliest Night of the Week," "Oh! What It Seemed to Be," "Five Minutes More," "I Dream of You," "Nancy," "Dream," "Day by Day," "Ol' Man River," and "Mam'selle."

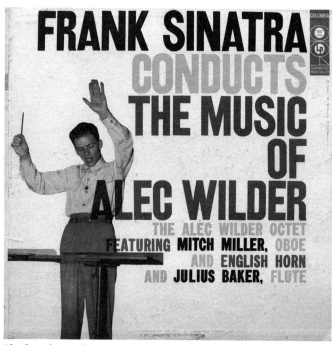

The first of several records with Sinatra conducting.

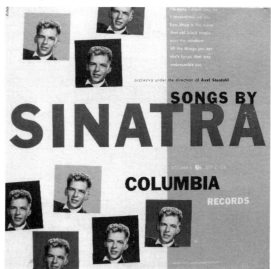

The first Sinatra albums held four 78 rpm records.

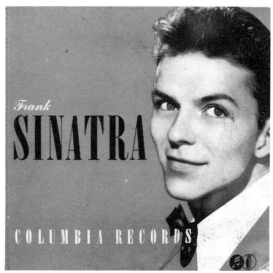

Through the years, Columbia has reissued and repackaged these recordings in a variety of ways, and their appeal and demand remain popular. *The Voice: The Columbia Years 1943–1952* was an ambitious six record/three cassette/four compact disc box set issued in 1986. It was followed in 1987 by *Hello Young Lovers* and *Christmas Dreaming*, and Columbia's album of *Sinatra Rarities* came out in 1988.

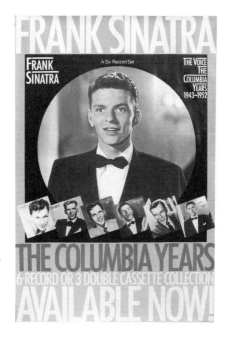

Promotional poster, 1986.

The 78 rpm record was popular for fifty years, but by the late 1950s, it was no longer being pressed.

"Ol' Man River" rolling along through the years at a variety of speeds: (from left) 78 rpm, 45 rpm, 33 rpm.

Sinatra's universal appeal exemplified by these 78 rpm pressings and

45 rpm single from Japan.

"Home on the Range" was issued on this Australian 78 rpm and "It All Came True" on this 78 rpm from England, but neither song was issued in the United States.

35

· The War Department and the Navy Department distributed Victory discs to entertain our WWII GI's.

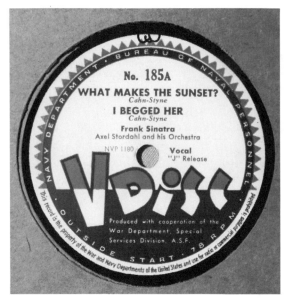

In addition to the regular issues, some collectors seek the promo copies.

"Hall of Fame Series" and the final days of the 78 rpm.

Columbia's 33 rpm microgroove single lost a battle for popularity against RCA's 45 rpm single with the large center hole.

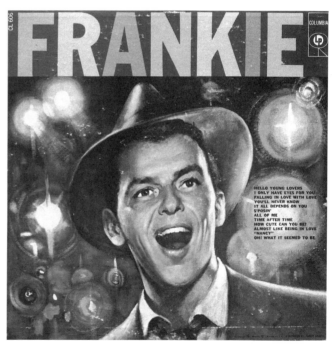

The first Columbia twelve-inch LP was issued with two different covers.

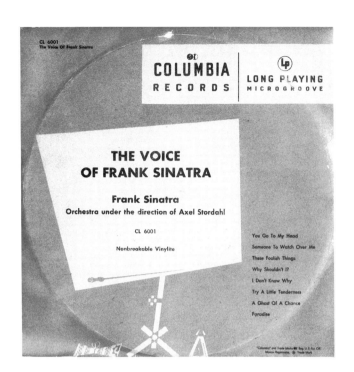

Ten-inch Long Playing Microgroove records made in the United States in the late 1940s and into the early 1950s.

Extended play records, USA.

SINATRA Sings Cole PORTER

I Concentrate On You
Why Can't You Behave
Why Shouldn't I?
You Do Something To Me

COLUMBIA

COLUMBIA

Sinatra sings Rodgers and Hart

WHERE OR WHEN
FALLING IN LOVE WITH LOVE
SPRING IS HERE
LOVER

Vol 2:
It All Depends On You   All Of Me
S'posin'   Time After Time

frankie

Hits from THE KING AND I

HELLO, YOUNG LOVERS   ROSEMARY CLOONEY
WE KISS IN A SHADOW   FRANK SINATRA
SOMETHING WONDERFUL   DORIS DAY
THE MARCH OF SIAMESE CHILDREN   PERCY FAITH

B-2515

I COULDN'T SLEEP A WINK LAST NIGHT
A LOVELY WAY TO SPEND AN EVENING
PEOPLE WILL SAY WE'RE IN LOVE
OH, WHAT A BEAUTIFUL MORNIN'

FRANK SINATRA

COLUMBIA HALL OF FAME series

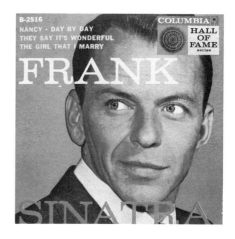

B-2516

NANCY · DAY BY DAY
THEY SAY IT'S WONDERFUL
THE GIRL THAT I MARRY

COLUMBIA HALL OF FAME series

FRANK SINATRA

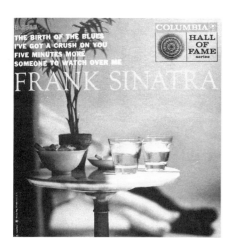

THE BIRTH OF THE BLUES
I'VE GOT A CRUSH ON YOU
FIVE MINUTES MORE
SOMEONE TO WATCH OVER ME

FRANK SINATRA

COLUMBIA HALL OF FAME series

B-2542

CASTLE ROCK
FAREWELL, FAREWELL TO LOVE
A LITTLE LEARNIN' IS
A DANG'ROUS THING

FRANK SINATRA
with HARRY JAMES & PEARL BAILEY

COLUMBIA HALL OF FAME series

B 2559

IF YOU ARE BUT A DREAM
I SHOULD CARE

FRANK SINATRA

COLUMBIA HALL OF FAME series

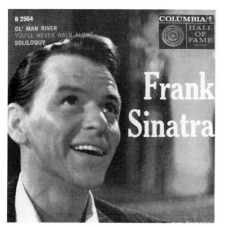

B 2564

OL' MAN RIVER
YOU'LL NEVER WALK ALONE
SOLILOQUY

Frank Sinatra

COLUMBIA HALL OF FAME series

B 2589 · SEPTEMBER SONG · AMONG MY
SOUVENIRS · THE THINGS WE DID LAST
SUMMER · OH, WHAT IT SEEMED TO BE
FRANK SINATRA

COLUMBIA HALL OF FAME series

B 2614

FRANK SINATRA

One for My Baby
If I Loved You
Put Your Dreams Away
You'll Never Know

COLUMBIA

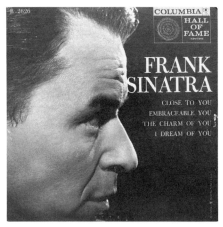
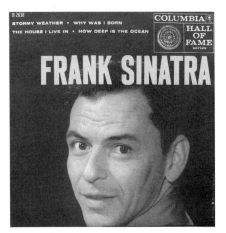

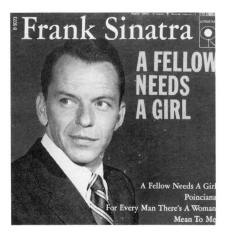

42

Extended play records, USA.

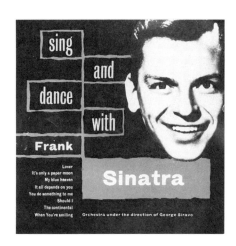

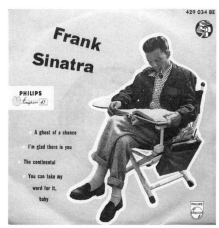

International pressings of Columbia recordings.

Frank Sinatra Favourites

You go to my head — April in Paris
How deep is the ocean — I've got a crush on you

fontana

LOVER

She's funny that way
Lover
Try a little tenderness
Laura

FRANK SINATRA

fontana

fontana

fontana

These Foolish Things
Fools Rush In
Paradise
I Don't Know Why

Fools rush in

FRANK SINATRA

Dream with Frank Sinatra

fontana

FOUR STAR SERIES

THE VOICE

FRANK SINATRA

(I don't stand)
A Ghost of A Chance With You
That Old Black Magic
Over the Rainbow
Spring is Here

fontana

FOUR STAR SERIES

FRANKIE!

FRANK SINATRA

She's Funny That Way
Birth Of The Blues
A Little Learnin' Is A Dang'rous Thing
(with PEARL BAILEY)

fontana

FRANK SINATRA

'The Song Is You'

Ain'tcha Ever Comin' Back
April In Paris
How Deep Is The Ocean
The Song Is You

fontana

fontana

'Bye, Baby!

Frank Sinatra

Should I?
Bye Bye Baby
Bim Bam Baby
You Do Something to Me

FIVE MINUTES MORE

FRANK SINATRA

fontana

FRANK SINATRA

Embraceable You

fontana

PHILIPS
Extended Play

LOVER
IT'S ONLY A PAPER MOON
MY BLUE HEAVEN
IT ALL DEPENDS ON YOU

SING and DANCE No. 2 with

FRANK SINATRA

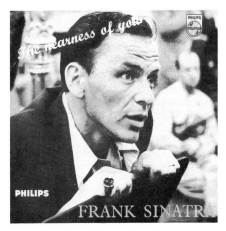

(Here and on facing page) International pressings of Columbia recordings.

9. **Higher and Higher**

(1943)

Belgian poster.

U.S. song sheet.

Song sheet from England.

Original one-sheet poster.

10. **Step Lively**

(1944)

One-sheet poster.

Song sheet from England.

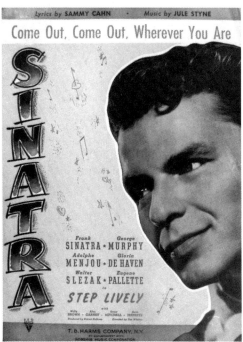

U.S. song sheet.

11. Magazines of the 1940s

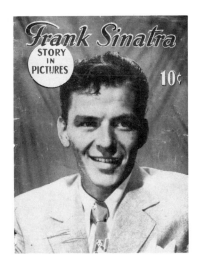
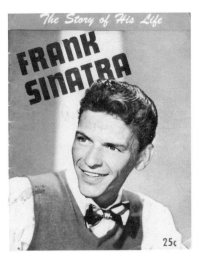
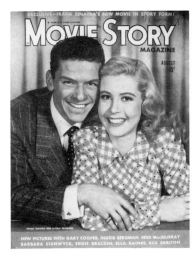

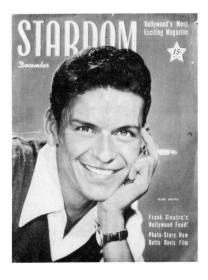

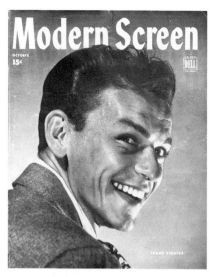

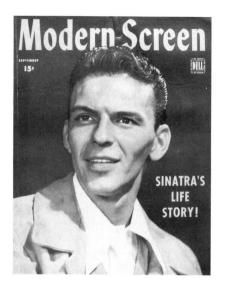

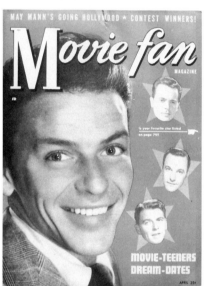

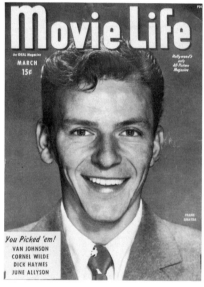

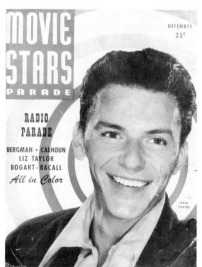

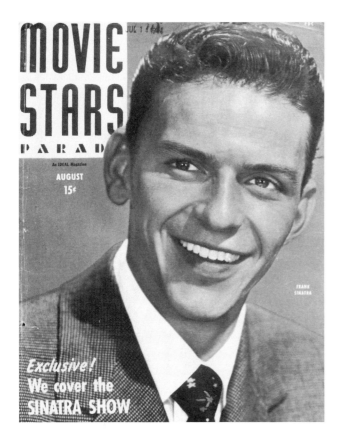

12. **Comic Books**

In addition to film adaptions, Sinatra has appeared in a variety of comic books.

First issue of *Junior Miss*, winter 1944, contains
Frank Sinatra's life story in comic form.

Frankenstein No. 1, summer 1945, contains parody character named "Frankie Singatra."

Young Life, summer 1945, features "Accentuate the Positive" essay on tolerance by Sinatra.

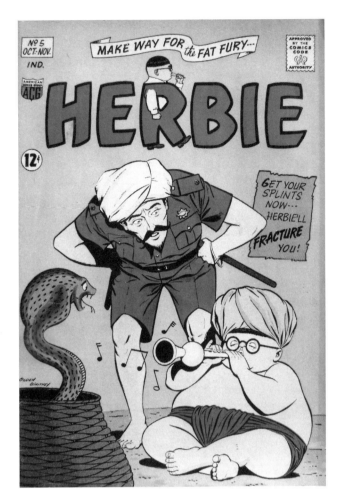

Herbie, 1964, has Frank and Dean appearance.

Keen Teens, 1945, with a ballot to vote for your favorite — Van Johnson or Frank Sinatra.

13. Sheet Music From the 1940s

Barton Music Corporation was a struggling music publishing company founded by ex-vaudevillian Ben Barton. A meeting in 1943 resulted in Frank becoming a partner in the business. Ben's daughter, Eileen, was to be a featured singer on Sinatra's Vimms Vitamins radio show.

It was common practice to picture an artist on the cover page to sell the sheet music. The artist did not have to record the song, nor was there any obligation to perform the song once. You may see song sheets with Sinatra's face on an unfamiliar title, and there are hundreds of these sheets with him pictured on the cover page.

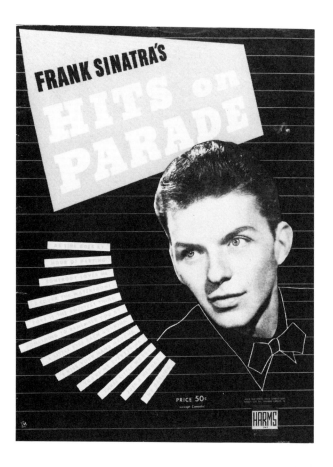

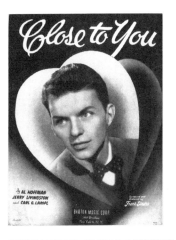

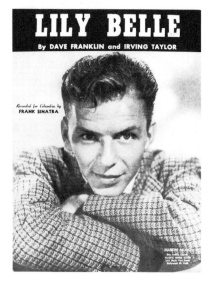

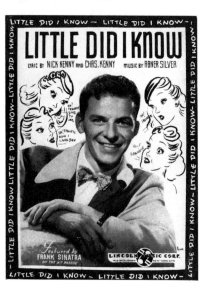

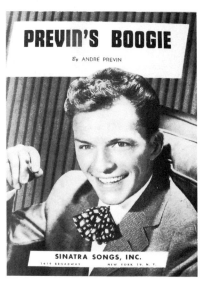

14. **Anchors Aweigh**

(1945)

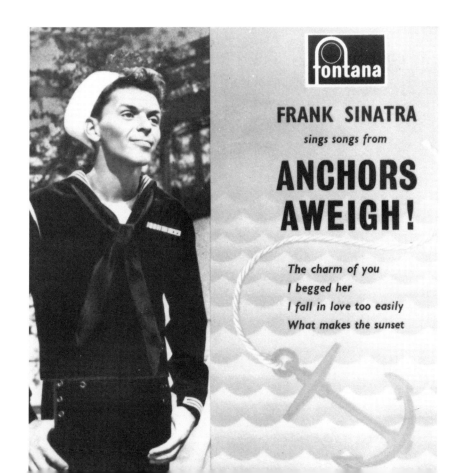

Magazine from England.

45 rpm EP from England.   57

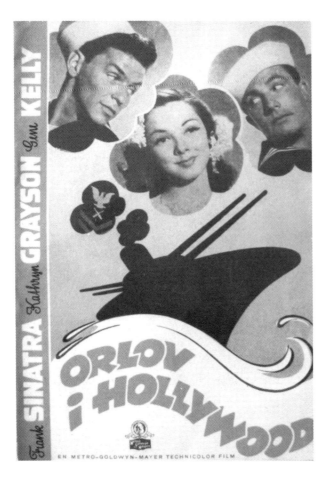

Danish programs.

French song sheet.

U.S. song sheet.

U.S. one-sheet printed in Spanish.

60

15. The House I Live In

(1945)

One-sheet poster.

Song sheet.

Lobby cards.

FOUR ONE-COLOR 11 x 14 LOBBY CARDS

From left, George Murphy, Peggy Ann Garner, and Frank with special Academy Award for *The House I Live In*.

16. Till the Clouds Roll By

(1 9 4 6)

A couple of ads.

Insert card measures 14 × 36 inches.

Production still of Frank singing Jerome Kern and Oscar Hammerstein II's "Ol' Man River."

17. **It Happened in Brooklyn**

(1947)

Half-sheet poster measures 22 × 28 inches.

One-sheet poster.

Ad.

Magazine for theater owners.

Song sheet.

Belgian poster.

18. **The Miracle of the Bells**

(1948)

Movie edition book.

Insert.

SNACK TRAY between scenes is welcomed by FRED MacMURRAY, VALLI and FRANK SINATRA. They're starring in film adaptation of Russell Janney's best-selling novel, *The Miracle of the Bells*, a Jesse L. Lasky-Walter MacEwen production. World Premiere Easter.

THESE BIG RKO PICTURES WILL SOON BE SHOWN AT YOUR THEATRE

den betagende
amerikanske storfilm

Klokkerne
ringer for dig

Program from Denmark.

19. **The Kissing Bandit**

(1948)

Song sheet.

British magazine.

One-sheet poster from Argentina.

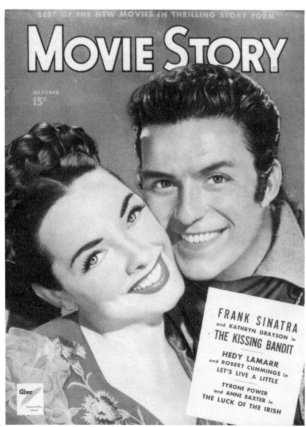

U.S. magazine.

Daughter Nancy visits *Bandit* set.

Frank and Gonzales.

This page from the original pressbook suggests promotional ideas.

71

20. Take Me Out to the Ball Game

(1949)

One-sheet poster.

Danish program.

Original ad.

Belgian poster.

21. **On the Town**

(1949)

January 1950 magazine.

Program from Denmark.

One-sheet poster.

Postcard from France.

22. Double Dynamite

(1951)

Sinatra has third billing and is not even pictured in the film's promotional artwork. The one sheet is shown here.

From left, Groucho Marx, Jane Russell, and Frank.

23. **Meet Danny Wilson**

(1951)

One-sheet poster.

Shelley Winters applies first aid after screen battle.

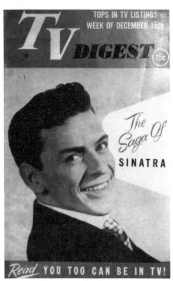

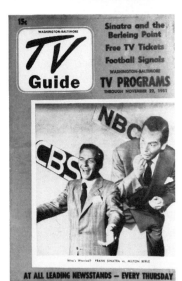

Early TV magazines.

24. Television 1950–1960

Sinatra's first television appearance was on Bob Hope's *Star Spangled Revue* for Frigidaire appliances. The ninety-minute variety show on NBC, May 27, 1950, featured Frank as a guest along with Peggy Lee and Beatrice Lillie. Hope's introduction of him:

It takes a lot of courage to get your feet wet in television. I'm really glad this chap finally decided to take the plunge — 'cause he's a guy that promotes a lot of fun wherever he's around. He's a great boy — the boy that made popular song history. I'm thrilled to introduce Mr. Frank Sinatra.

A young blue eyes sang "Come Rain or Come Shine" on that live broadcast from New York, and he took part in a couple of comedy skits. One, titled "The Road to Frigidaire," had Frank playing a pipe-smoking, big-eared character named Bing Crosby. Milton Berle put in a cameo appearance, all making a grand introductory showcase for Sinatra in the new medium.

Sinatra did not fare as well on television as he did with films, records, radio, and live performances. Several "specials" approach brilliance, but a Sinatra series never met critical success. His first series, *The Frank Sinatra Show*, premiered October 7, 1950, just a few months after his appearance with Bob Hope. Starting as a half-hour variety show for Bulova watches, it added Echo housewares as a sponsor in 1951 and expanded to an hour. Axel Stordahl was the show's musical director, and his wife June Hutton appeared regularly to share the vocal chores with Frank. The guest list for the series was impressive: Sarah Vaughan, Jackie Gleason, Phil Silvers, Basil Rathbone, Rudy Vallee, Frank Fontaine, Jack Benny, Louis Armstrong, The Three Stooges, Buster Keaton, Ben Blue, Sammy Davis, Jr., James Mason, and Liberace — all now gone. Sinatra handled the comic routines well, but they just were not funny, no matter how many foolish costumes he donned. The

Early TV magazines.

songs, as always, were just fine. The laughter enjoyed on the radio was absent, and the songs alone weren't enough to make the series successful. The ratings battles against the hugely popular Milton Berle came to an abrupt end when Sinatra's now sponsor-less show was dropped June 1, 1952.

The next year, Sinatra made several guest appearances on Berle's show, and on NBC's special broadcast honoring Berle on March 26, 1978, Sinatra paid tribute to Uncle Miltie by saying "he paved the way."

A highlight of the Sinatra years on television was a musical version by Sammy Cahn and Jimmy Van Heusen of Thornton Wilder's *Our Town*. Frank took the narrative role of the "stage manager" and costarred with Paul Newman and Eva Marie Saint. The show, which aired September 19, 1955, was one of the early color broadcasts, and one of the songs from it was "Love and Marriage," which won an Emmy and became a big hit for Sinatra.

In forty years of television, Sinatra had only one more series. Sponsored by Chesterfield cigarettes one week, alternating with the Bulova watch company again, this was a series of half-hour musicals and dramas. It premiered October

18, 1957, with an hour show. Bob Hope was a guest, along with Peggy Lee (another Capitol recording star), and Kim Novak (Frank's *Man With the Golden Arm* and *Pal Joey* costar). After twenty-one half-hour musicals and ten thirty-minute dramas, the series ended June 27, 1958. The single-season series' guest list included: Dean Martin, Bing Crosby, Dinah Shore, Robert Mitchum, Louis Prima and Keely Smith, Stan Freberg, Jo Stafford, Shirley Jones, Sammy Davis, Jr., Van Johnson, Joey Bishop, Eddie Fisher, Spike Jones, Ethel Merman, Ella Fitzgerald, and Natalie Wood.

Critics claimed Sinatra appeared unrehearsed. Little did it matter that an unrehearsed Sinatra performs far better than others who labor over their material for hours on end. Others felt the show tried to be too "hip." Tapes of these half-hour shows (only a handful are known to exist) are among the most sought by video collectors. The audio portions, however, exist for nearly the entire series.

The next season, Sinatra did four specials on ABC for Timex. The fourth was "Welcome Home, Elvis," with Presley making his first appearance after his Army gig. Sammy Davis, Jr., Joey Bishop, and Peter Lawford also

79

appeared, giving the viewer a taste of "the clan's" Vegas act, and Frank's daughter Nancy joined the festivities. Elvis broke in two newly-recorded songs and sang "Witchcraft" to Sinatra's version of "Love Me Tender." Bishop joked that it would have been cheaper to present World War II than pay Elvis's fee. The ratings for the May 12, 1960, broadcast set a five-year record.

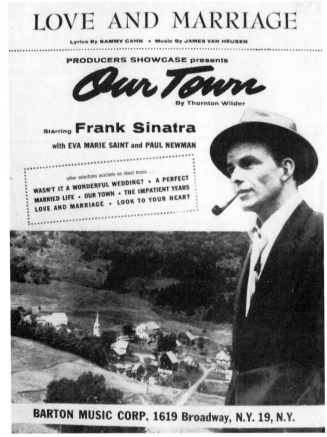

Hit song from *Our Town*.

Sinatra had a weekly CBS Television series on October 1950 through June 1952.

8:00 ④ ⑧ ⑪ PRODUCERS' SHOWCASE
OUR TOWN by Thornton Wilder
starring

| Frank SINATRA | Eva Marie SAINT | Paul NEWMAN | Paul HARTMAN | Ernest TRUEX | Sylvia FIELD |

music by James VAN HEUSEN • lyrics by Sammy CAHN

[COLOR] "Our Town," 17 years old now, has become a musical. David Shaw has adapted the script. The songs have been written by James Van Heusen and Sammy Cahn.

Sinclair Lewis familiarized a generation of Americans with a satiric view of the American small town. Wilder's play reverses the trend, and takes a loving look at the inhabitants of the typical town of Grover's Corners. The plot is pegged on the lives of a boy and a girl in the town, and follows them through romance, marriage and death.

Act 1: It's May 1901. The act opens at dawn on a street in Grover's Corners. The cameras rove through the Gibbs' and Webbs' homes and the office of the Grover's Corners Sentinel.
Songs: "Our Town"..."Grover's Corners"..."The Impatient Years."
Act 2: Now it's July 1904. Again we enter the Gibbs' and Webbs' homes, then travel to an area near the school, the drugstore soda fountain and the church.
Songs: "Love and Marriage"..."A Perfect Married Life"..."The Impatient Years" (reprise) ..."Wasn't It A Wonderful Wedding?"
Act 3: Nine years have passed. It's summer 1913. The scene is the cemetery. Flashbacks take us back to 1899. We return to the town in 1913, where the play closes.
Song: "Look to Your Heart."

Cast

Stage Mgr. (Mr. Morgan)	Frank Sinatra
Emily Webb	Eva Marie Saint
George Gibbs	Paul Newman
Dr. Gibbs	Ernest Truex
Mrs. Gibbs	Sylvia Field
Editor Webb	Paul Hartman
Mrs. Webb	Peg Hillias
Mrs. Soames	Carol Veazie

Credits: PRODUCER: Fred Coe. DIRECTOR: Delbert Mann. CHOREOGRAPHY: Valerie Bettis. SETS: Otis Riggs. COSTUMES: Robert Campbell.

A-22   TV GUIDE

Our Town cast rehearsal: Paul Newman, Eva Marie Saint, Sinatra.

A variety of costumes wasn't enough to beat Milton Berle in the ratings.

81

DOWN BEAT

Carefree

New York—A recent rehearsal for his CBS video show found Frank Sinatra looking pretty jovial. Tis said he's lopped some 13 points from Milton Berle's viewer rating already, and the program has been showing constant improvement. The Voice's divorce from wife Nancy was granted on Oct. 30 in Santa Monica, leaving him free for his expected marriage to Ava Gardner.

MALE SINGERS—NOT BAND	
Billy Eckstine	294
Perry Como	44
Frankie Laine	43
Frank Sinatra	40
Nat Cole	35
Louis Armstrong	32
Bing Crosby	31
Mel Torme	29
Herb Jeffries	21
Tony Bennett	20
Bill Farrell	9
Tony Martin	9
Bob Eberly	8
Guy Mitchell	8
Art Lund	6
Dick Haymes	5
Mario Lanza	5
Gordon MacRae	5

(None Under 5 Listed)

ON THE SET WITH SINATRA

"Like your pleasure big? Come on in and find yourself a seat.

"We're on for Chesterfield every Friday night, ABC-TV.

"We've got music, drama, loads of stars!

"It all adds up to big, big pleasure . . .

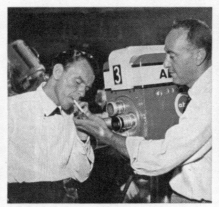

like you get in Chesterfield.

"You can tell with one drag . . . You're smoking smooth—smoking clean!

"This is satisfaction—man-size satisfaction! Chesterfield!

"Ready to roll? Hold on. How can I do the show when this pack's empty!"

Chesterfield presents Frank Sinatra, ABC-TV Friday nights— Live Première October 18 **Full Hour**

CHESTERFIELD

© Liggett & Myers Tobacco Company

KING and REGULAR

Sinatra's second television series was on ABC 1957–58, sponsored by Chesterfield cigarettes.

Sinatra special to "Welcome Home, Elvis" from the Army, in May 1960 set five-year ratings record.

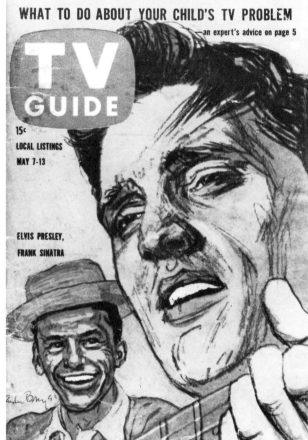

One of the most difficult *TV Guide* issues to find is sought by Elvis and Sinatra collectors alike.

25. **From Here to Eternity**

(1953)

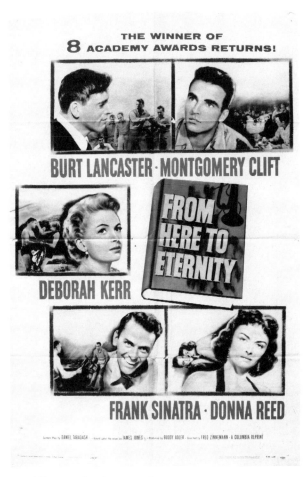

Two different style reissue one-sheets.

Song sheet for another Sinatra hit.

A 45 rpm record from Germany.

Private Maggio publicity photo.

Montgomery Clift holds Sinatra back from Ernest Borgnine. Sinatra wins Academy Award as Best Supporting Actor.

One-sheet poster from Argentina.

26. **Suddenly**

(1 9 5 4)

Belgian poster.

Model Trains Setting Will Dramatize Sensational Story!

This suggested set-piece, in 3 dimensions and using an actual set of running model trains, can be set up in your lobby, in department store window or in any window where model trains are sold. Additional effect can be achieved by putting Sinatra figure under blue spot with strong light on train and station. Flasher light behind copy and star and title names will further animate the display.

Art for Sinatra figure available as "Still SL-Art 8" from National Screen.

From *Suddenly* pressbook.   89

27. Young at Heart

(1954)

Song sheet.

Program from Denmark.

From Spain.

Life-Like Cutout For Display

Here's a standee suggestion for lobbies which can easily be made up by blowing up Standee Still 398-Ad Art A. Pick up billing and title from ads — let your sign painter do the rest.

Life-like cutout for display.

Ten-inch LP from England.

28. **Not As a Stranger**

(1955)

Magazine ad.

One-sheet poster.

29. The Tender Trap

(1 9 5 5)

Frank **Sinatra**

Debbie **Reynolds**

David **Wayne**

Celeste **Holm**

UNGKARL I FÆLDEN

OPTAGET I **CinemaScope** OG FARVE

Program from Denmark.

Frank, Joey Fay, and David Wayne relax after a day's shooting.

30. **Guys and Dolls**

(1955)

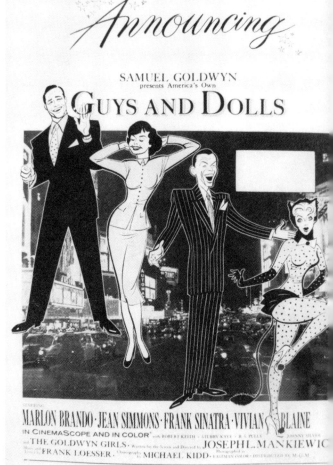

Movie edition pocketbook.

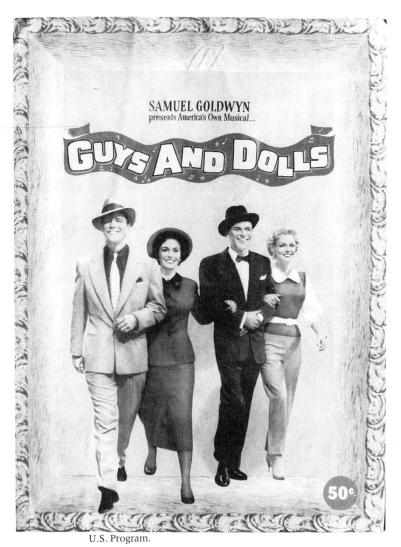

U.S. Program.

From a Sweden pressbook.

Contractual agreements with Capitol prevented a soundtrack LP from being issued, but a Marlon Brando/Jean Simmons EP without Sinatra was released by Decca.

95

31. The Man With the Golden Arm

(1955)

Argentine one-sheet.

Belgian poster.

Movie edition pocketbook.

French comic book.

45 rpm EP from Germany.

32. **Capitol Records**

(1953–1960)

Promotional coasters from Japan.

Full page ad from December 4, 1965 *Cash Box*.

Many record collectors think of a different Sinatra on Capitol Records, distinctive as the red Columbia label is from the purple Capitol one. The end of the Columbia period is definitive as the curtain between acts. A new Sinatra emerged from his "low period" with a confidence, a maturity, a cockiness, an arrogance in the voice not present in the earlier years. Perhaps it was the "comeback" with an Academy Award for *From Here to Eternity*. Maybe it was new management, a chance to work with a new recording company, or an opportunity to work with new arrangers. Whatever the reasons, most agree these were his finest years.

The first Capitol recording session, April 2, 1953, resulted in four songs. "Lean Baby," backed with "I'm Walking Behind You," were

Seven-inch 33 rpm compact double.

the first issued (Capitol 2450). Belated releasing is one aspect of fascination to the collector, and this first session is a classic example. A third song from the session, "Don't Make a Beggar of Me," was not issued until the 1965 release of the *Forever Frank* LP. A fourth, "Day In, Day Out," was issued for the first time in 1987 on *The Point of No Return* CD, and never issued on record.

Frank's recordings for Capitol have been reissued, repackaged, remixed, and have remitted handsome sums to the company coffers. In fall 1990, in celebration of Sinatra's seventy-fifth birthday, a package of seventy-five tracks was issued as *The Capitol Years*.

Seven-inch 33 rpm record for jukeboxes.

Promotional poster from England.

Ten-inch 78 rpm records in sleeves.

The first Sinatra single for Capitol.

In celebration of Frank's seventy-fifth Birthday, seventy-five Sinatra tracks were released in deluxe package called *The Capitol Years*.

Sinatra looking away from lovers.

Sinatra looking at lovers. Collectors want both covers.

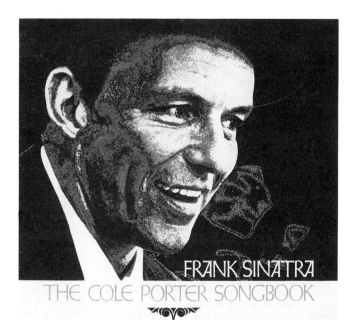

Argentina

Australia

Australia

England

England

England

England

International LPs:

England

102

England

England

France

Germany

Germany

Holland

Italy

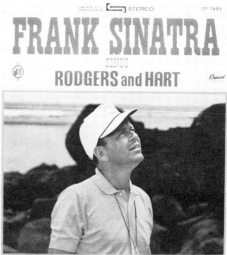

Japan

Japan

Japan

Japan

Japan

International LPs:

New Zealand

104

Bulgaria

England

England

England

England

England

England

England

England

England

England

England

England

England

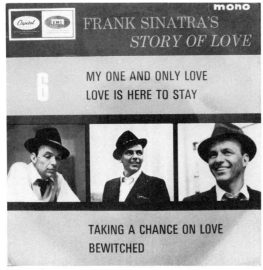

England

England

England

England

England

France

Germany

Holland

Italy

Italy

107

Italy

Italy

Italy

Italy

Japan

Japan

United States

United States

United States

United States

United States

United States

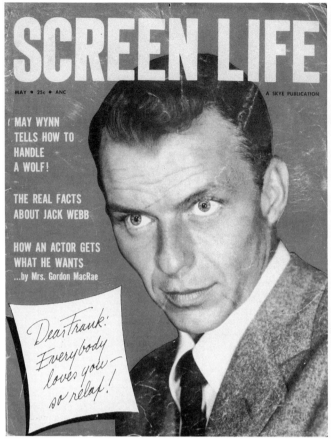

RECORDS HI-FI

March 11, 1953

WORL

DOWN BEAT

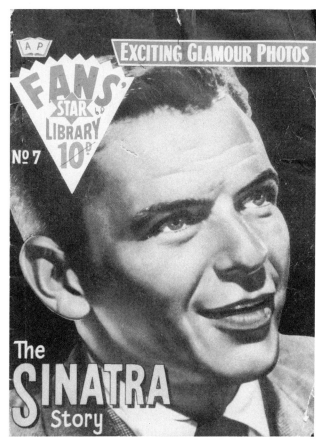

AP

FANS' STAR LIBRARY
Nº 7
10d

EXCITING GLAMOUR PHOTOS

The SINATRA Story

LARGEST CIRCULATION OF ANY SONG MAGAZINE

MORE PAGES — MORE FEATURES

HIT PARADER

JULY 25c
1954

A CHARLTON PUBLICATION

WANTED
JILTED
THE MAN WITH THE BANJO
HERE
OH THAT'LL BE JOYFUL
ANEMA E CORE
IT HAPPENS TO BE ME
IF YOU LOVE ME
A GIRL A GIRL
I SPEAK TO THE STARS
ALONE TOO LONG
THERE'LL BE NO TEARDROPS TONIGHT
THE KID'S LAST FIGHT
CRAZY MIXED UP SONG
ANGELA MIA
GOING LIKE WILDFIRE
THE HAPPY WANDERER
MAYBE NEXT TIME
SUCH A NIGHT

FRANK SINATRA

Exclusive Features
"Rhythm Is My Beat" by Teresa Brewer
Candid Close-up Of The Richard Haymans
Spotting The Stars — Quiz

What I learned about TV — Sinatra

METRONOME

MAY, 1951 35c

BANDS   RECORDS
RADIO   TELEVISION
SINGERS   MOVIES

PERRY COMO
FRANKIE LAINE
FRANK SINATRA

ALL BALL PLAYERS ARE AFRAID—BY BIRDIE TEBBETTS

LOOK

15¢ MAY 14, 1957

The life of
FRANK
SINATRA
Talent
and tantrums

LOOK

I'll beat Rocky
by Archie Moore

What's behind the
Ike—Truman feud?

15¢ SEPTEMBER 6, 1955

7 COLOR PAGES OF
RECORDING STARS

FRANK SINATRA

METRONOME
MUSIC USA

DECEMBER, 1957 35¢

Johnny Richards
Tony Scott
Nat Hentoff
The Bass
Toscanini
Records
High-Fidelity

Frank Sinatra:
Mr. Personality
(see page 14)

Sheet Music of the 1950s

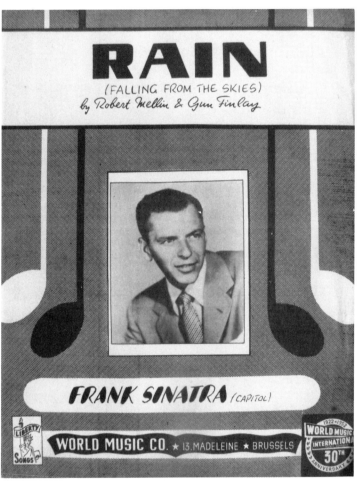

113

114

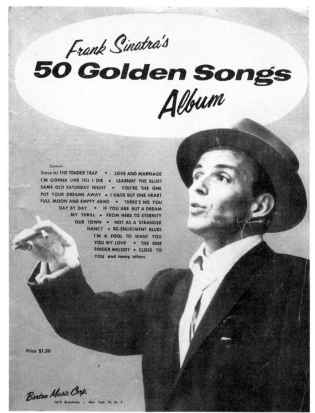

35. **Johnny Concho**

(1956)

Movie edition pocketbook.

U.S. pressbook.

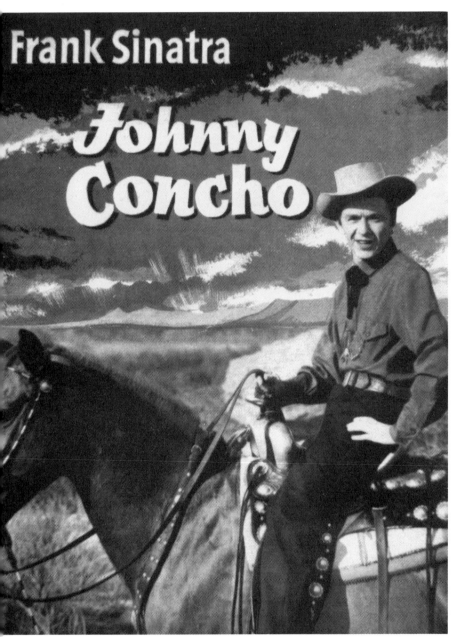

Danish program.

Belgian poster.

117

36. **High Society**

(1956)

Belgian poster.

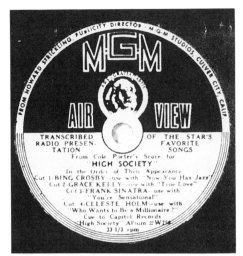

Special disc for radio promotion.

Song sheet for the Academy Award-winning "True Love."

Frank with Bing Crosby and Grace Kelly between scenes.

Box set of 45 rpm EPs.

37. Around the World in 80 Days

(1956)

Board game, Sinatra pictured fourth up on right.

Movie edition
pocketbook.

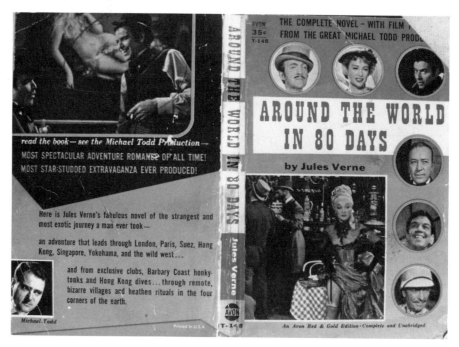

With George Raft in *80 Days*.

Comic book.
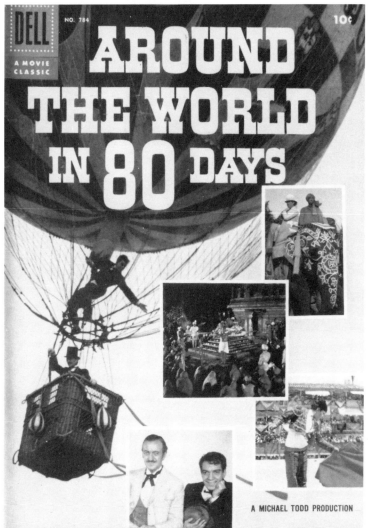

38. The Pride and the Passion

(1957)

Belgian poster.

U.S. comic book.

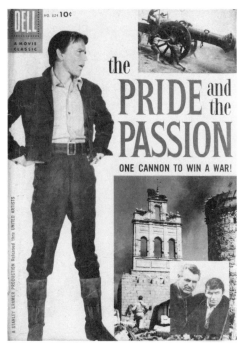

122

French comic book.

Movie edition pocketbook.

U.S. one-sheet.

Italian lobby poster.

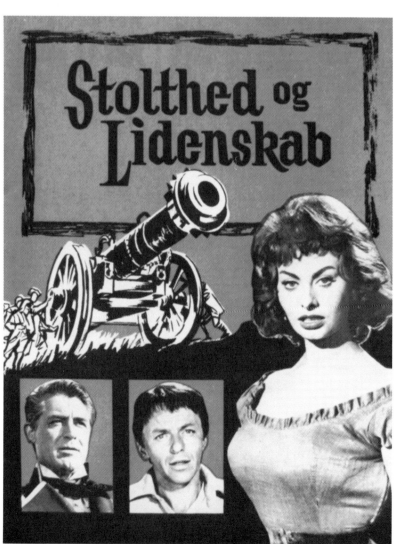

Danish program.

39. **The Joker Is Wild**

(1957)

Poster from Belgium.

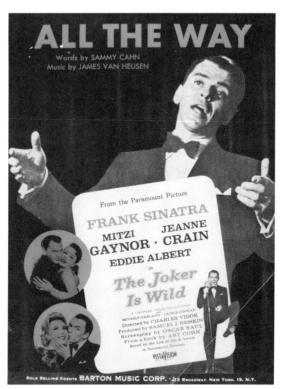

Sheet music for Academy Award-
winning song.

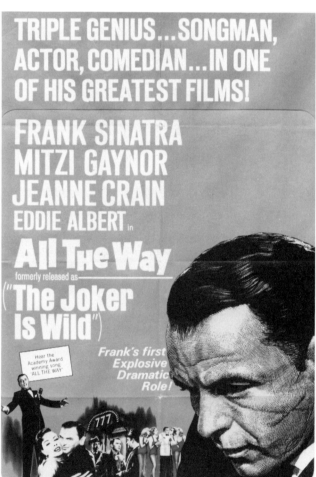

With success of the song, *Joker* was rereleased as *All the Way*. This is the one-sheet.

40. **Pal Joey**

(1957)

Sheet music from England.

One sheet from Argentina.

41. **Kings Go Forth**

(1958)

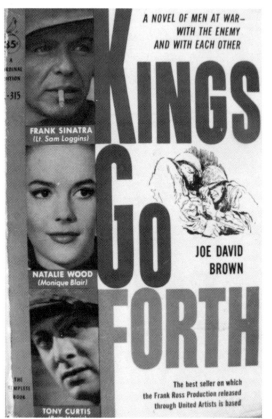

Movie edition pocketbook from the U.S.

Danish program.

The soundtrack LP.

128

Sinatra makes Tony Curtis an offer he can't refuse.

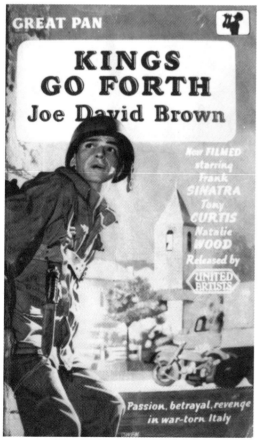

Lobby card.

Movie edition pocketbook from England.

129

42. **Some Came Running**

(1958)

Original Argentine poster.

Program from world premiere.

Soundtrack LP.

Reissue Argentine poster.

Frank and Dean in scene from *Some Came Running.*

Between scenes of *Some Came Running.*

French comic book.

Original Danish program.

Reissue Danish program.

43. **A Hole in the Head**

(1959)

One-sheet from Argentina.

Program from Denmark.

Movie edition pocketbook.

134

44. **Never So Few**

(1959)

As Steve McQueen's fame grew, so did his billing and his presence on these Argentine posters.

Films and Filming magazine from England.

136

Danish programs.

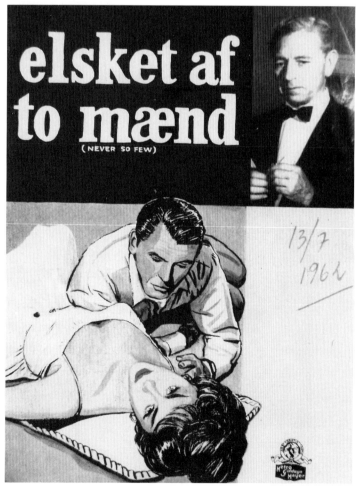

137

45. **Can-Can**

(1960)

U.S. one-sheet.

Song sheet from England.

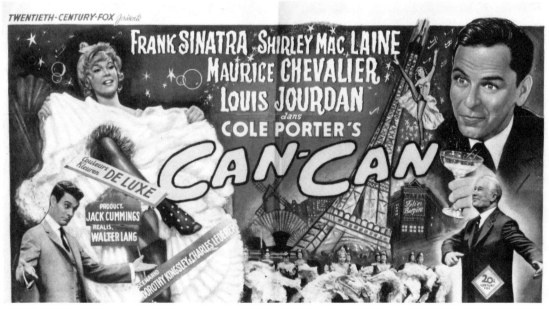

Belgian poster.

Nikita Khrushchev visits
Can-Can set.

Sinatra with Maurice Chevalier. That's
Shirley MacLaine under the table.

46. **Ocean's Eleven**

(1960)

Belgian posters.

$11 bill giveaway.

140

47. **Pepe**

(1960)

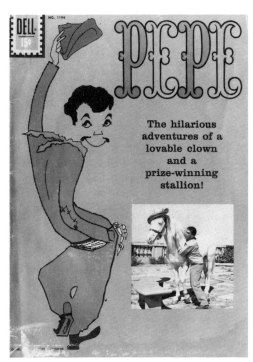

Comic book.

One-sheet poster with a star "reserved for Frank Sinatra."

48. **Reprise Records**

(1960–1970)

The Columbia years totaled eleven (including the 1939 recordings with Harry James). The Capitol years were 1953 through 1961, just nine. The Reprise years began in 1960 and continue into the 1990s, producing, by far, the bulk of the Sinatra record library.

Early Reprise advertising described him as "a newer, happier, emancipated Sinatra . . . untrammeled, unfettered, unconfined." Over the years there have been many Reprise ad campaigns to promote a variety of Sinatra product associated with the label. From the 1960 recording sessions of *Ring-A-Ding Ding* to the 1990 release of *The Reprise Collection*, these are the "very good years."

Special projects included an album of Americana and another of Christmas songs with Bing Crosby and Fred Waring.

Sinatra's first Reprise LP (1960).

"The Reprise Repertory Theatre" company included Dean Martin, Bing Crosby, Sammy Davis, Jr., Dinah Shore, Debbie Reynolds, and a stable full of front runners.

142

Sinatra Family Christmas Album, pressed in Spain.

Reprise promotional ad.

An album recorded in England June 1962, issued in several countries but never the United States.

British issue not available in the United States.

The Reprise label as it should appear. Mechanical error produces an interesting collectible.

143

Reprise LP 1023 never released.

Souvenir 45 rpm from Cal-Neva Lodge.

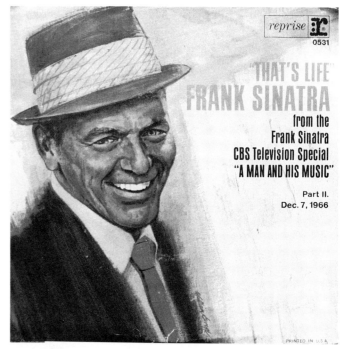

Singles issued in the U.S.

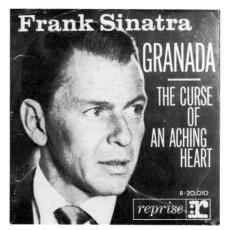

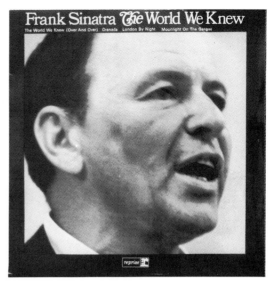

145

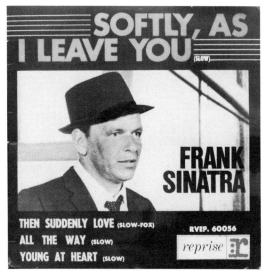

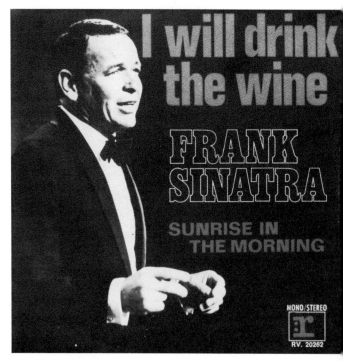

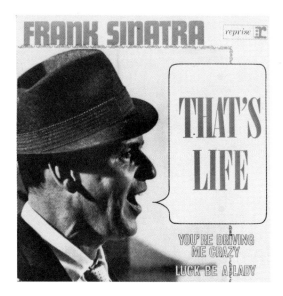

146

GERMANY

GERMANY

GERMANY

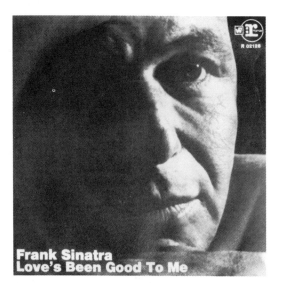

JAPAN

JAPAN

JAPAN

JAPAN

JAPAN

SPAIN

SPAIN

49. **The Devil at 4 O'Clock**

(1961)

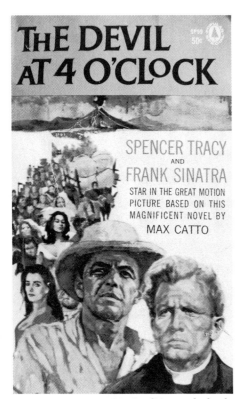

Movie edition pocketbook.

Record from Italy.

Lobby card.

Lobby card.

50. **Sergeants 3**

(1962)

Danish program.

British quad-sheet (30 × 40 inches).

Record from Italy.

51. **The Road to Hong Kong**

(1962)

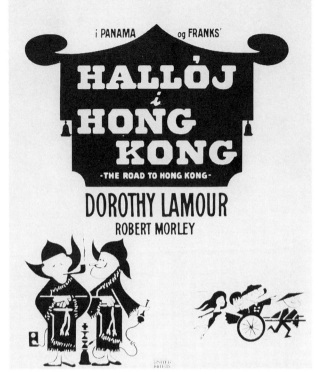

Danish program.

Frank and Dean land for a brief appearance in Bing and Bob's final "Road" film.

One-sheet poster.

154

52. The Manchurian Candidate

(1962)

U.S. "teaser" displayed prior to film opening.

Belgian poster.

Danish program.

One-sheet.

53. **Come Blow Your Horn**

(1963)

Poster from Belgium.

Half-sheet poster from the U.S.

Program from Denmark.

A pinch from Tony Bill and a punch from
Dan Blocker.

Record from Italy.

157

54. The List of Adrian Messenger

(1963)

Giant lobby standee.

Program from Denmark.

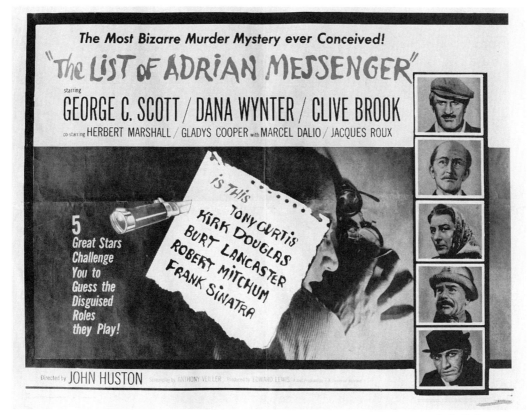

The half-sheet poster.

55. **4 for Texas**

(1964)

Reissue poster from Spain.

Danish program.

Lobby card.

German poster.

Lobby poster from Italy.

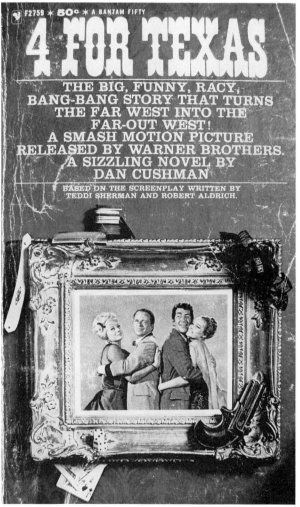

Movie version pocketbook.

56. **Robin and the 7 Hoods**

(1964)

Lobby display ad in pressbook.

Belgian poster.

His kind of town.

With Barbara Rush.

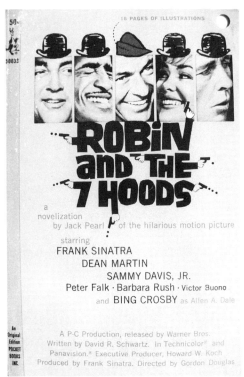

Movie edition pocketbook.

Robin and his band of merry women.

Color check before filming.

57. **None But the Brave**

(1965)

Poster from Belgium.

Half-sheet poster
from the U.S.

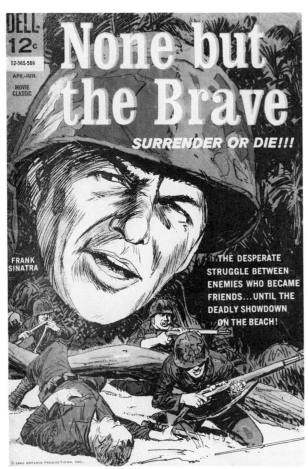

Comic book.

Movie edition pocketbook.

58. Von Ryan's Express

(1965)

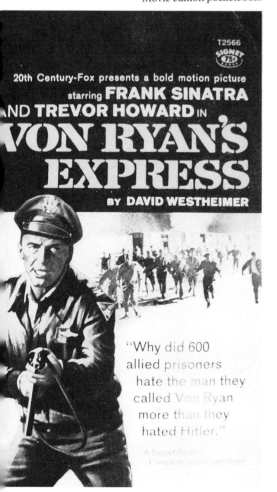

Movie edition pocketbook.

Danish program.

45 rpm single from Italy.

Is this *Laugh-In*'s Arte Johnson? Very interesting!

Sheet music for piano.

59. **Marriage on the Rocks**

(1965)

U.S. one-sheet.

British display.

Movie edition pocketbook.

Danish program.

British lobby cards.

60. **Magazines of the 1960s**

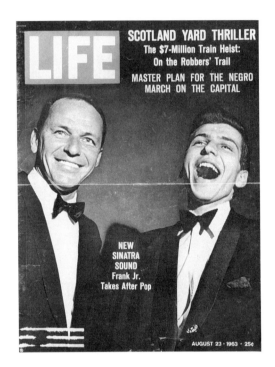

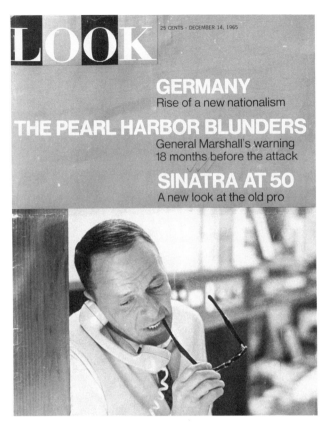

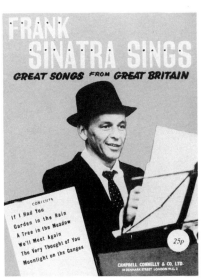

62. Television 1965–1970

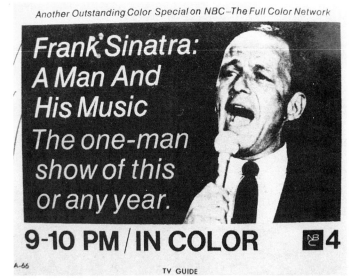

Another Outstanding Color Special on NBC—The Full Color Network

Frank Sinatra:
A Man And
His Music
The one-man
show of this
or any year.

9-10 PM / IN COLOR NBC 4

TV GUIDE

Award-winning special airs Thanksgiving 1965.

Nearing fifty, a reflective Sinatra recorded "The September of My Years," but there were no signs of slowing down. He made three films in 1965, and it was also "A Very Good Year" for Sinatra on television. He appeared on the opening show of Dean Martin's NBC series on September 16. A month later, he hosted ABC's *The Hollywood Palace* and performed a mini-concert with Count Basie. On November 16, he was the focus of CBS's special hour documentary, "Sinatra: An American Original," hosted by Walter Cronkite. The Emmy-winning *A Man and His Music* aired on Thanksgiving Day. He also found time to appear on *The Soupy Sales Show* and take some pie in the face with William B. Williams, Trini Lopez, and Sammy Davis, Jr.

A Man and His Music was the first of five specials sponsored by Budweiser. It was a pure hour of Sinatra — no comedians, no dancers, no guests, and none needed. Reprise released an ambitious double-album retrospective narrated by Sinatra with the same title as the television special. *A Man and His Music Part II* aired in December 1966, and daughter Nancy was the guest. The following year there was *A Man and His Music + Ella + Jobim*, and 1968 brought *Francis Albert Sinatra Does His Thing*. The 1969 special, simply titled *Sinatra* returned to the one-man-show format, but without the critical acclaim of its predecessor.

Special deluxe set by Reprise for Sinatra's fiftieth Birthday.

A Man And His Music Part II airs December 1966. Budweiser gave this Reprise promotional LP to its better accounts. The songs on this LP are available on other Sinatra albums, but the great cover photo makes this highly desirable.

173

Francis Albert Sinatra Does His Thing, the
fourth Budweiser special, airs November 25,
1968, on CBS.

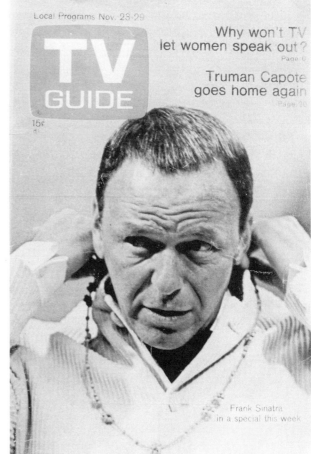

A Man And His Music is repeated May 1966.

Frank and Dean guest on Bing Crosby's 1965 special.

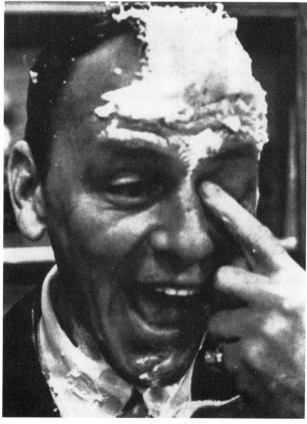

Frank takes a pie in the face on *The Soupy Sales Show,*
1965.

63. **Cast a Giant Shadow**

(1966)

Vince and a seltzer bottle —
two things that scream on their
way down.

64. Assault on a Queen

(1966)

One-sheet.

Movie edition pocketbook.

65. **The Naked Runner**

(1967)

New Zealand counter display promoting the book.

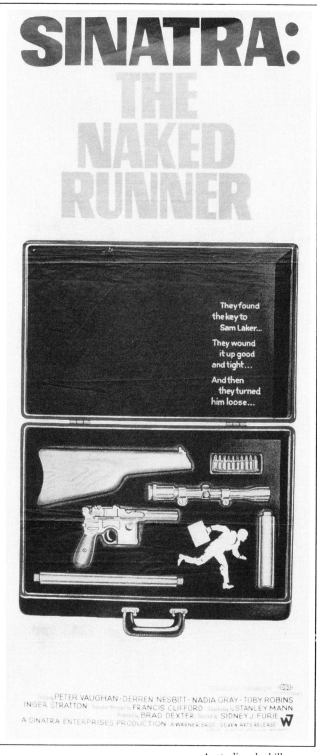

Australian daybill poster.

178

Movie edition pocketbook.

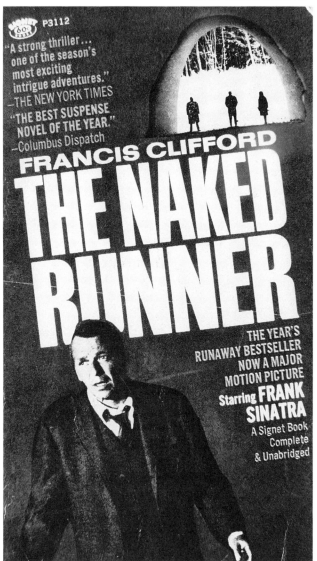

British pressbook.

66. Tony Rome

(1967)

Program from Denmark.

180

Poster from Belgium.

Ad from French magazine.

181

67. **The Detective**

(1968)

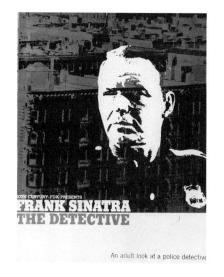

An adult look at a police detective

Danish program.

Selected scenes
on 8mm home movie.

68. **Lady in Cement**

(1968)

British theater handout.

Danish program.

69. **Dirty Dingus Magee**

(1970)

U.S. insert.

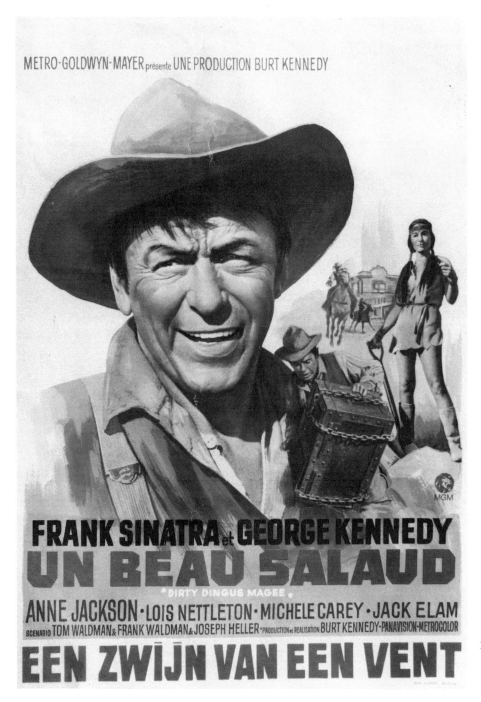

Belgian poster.

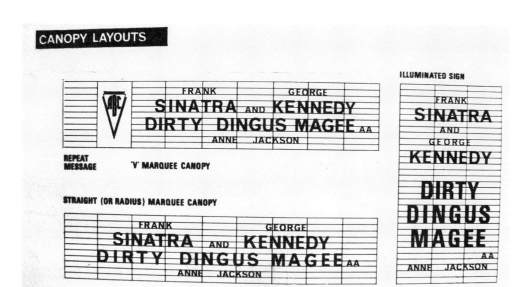

U.S. one-sheet.

British lobby card.

British poster.

British pressbook for *Dingus* and *The Extraordinary Seaman*.

70. The Retirement — 1971

The heralded self-imposed "retirement" may have resulted from poor sales of the *A Man Alone* and *Watertown* LPs in 1969. Certainly, *Dirty Dingus Magee* did not add to the prestige of Sinatra's film career. The fifth Budweiser TV special, simply titled *Sinatra*, could not approach the mastery of *A Man and His Music* four years earlier, nor did it enjoy that show's critical success. Maybe he was just tired and needed a break from the pace he'd kept up since 1935. Most likely, it was a combination of factors. Sinatra announced he would retire from public life.

The Ahmanson Theatre in Los Angeles supplied what was to be the final stage. If Sinatra only wanted a break from the routine, publicity for the concert to benefit the Motion Picture and Television Relief Fund's Fiftieth Anniversary indicated a farewell appearance. On June 13, 1971, in a literal puff of smoke, he closed, imploring his audience to "excuse me while I disappear."

Other than the occasional photo on the golf course with friends Bob Hope and then Vice-President Spiro Agnew, Sinatra was out of the show-biz limelight.

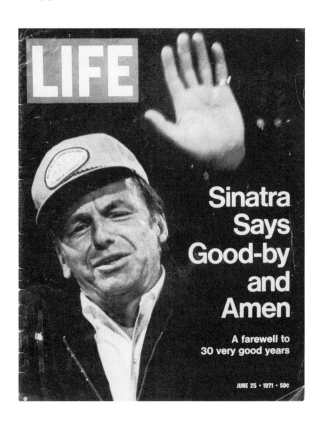

189

71. Ol' Blue Eyes Is Back — 1973

The "retirement" was but a brief respite. Bob Hope emceed a Republican fund-raiser at the Lyric Theatre, Baltimore, on May 20, 1972. As last star on the bill, Sinatra walked to the microphone, the audience expecting a few spoken words. "This is ridiculous. I haven't worked in a year." He than sang "The Gentleman Is a Champ," a parody of "The Lady Is a Tramp," in tribute to Spiro Agnew. Additional political rallies followed, and by April 17, 1973, Sinatra was performing at the White House. President Richard Nixon, in his introduction, said "Sinatra is to the world of entertainment what the Washington Monument is to Washington — he's the top."

Ol' Blue Eyes Is Back! not only was more than a clever promotional phrase but also the title of his new NBC television special for Magnavox (aired November 18, 1973) and his new record album for Reprise. Released in October, the LP included the appropriate "Let Me Try Again," a French song with new lyrics by Paul Anka and Sammy Cahn.

Sinatra, at age fifty-eight, was making his first nightclub appearance in three years and "Ol' Blue Eyes" was back at Caesars Palace in Las Vegas for a January 25, 1974, opening. Daughter Tina would wed Wes Farrell the next day at a Caesars' penthouse ceremony. Frank would return to Caesars that June for an engagement with Ella Fitzgerald and in September for a week with daughter Nancy and son Frank, Jr.

Sinatra was also back on the big screen as he introduced the opening segments in MGM's *That's Entertainment!* in spring 1974. He then opened an April tour at Carnegie Hall, and went on to play Providence, Detroit, Philadelphia, Washington, D.C., and Chicago.

July 1974 saw a tour in Japan and Australia, highlighted by the infamous Melbourne monolog. Another U.S. tour in October included Boston, Buffalo, Philadelphia, and New York's Madison Square Garden concert that was broadcast live by ABC on October 13. Billed as "The

Record from France "Let Me Try Again."

190

Main Event," this would also be the title of his third LP for Reprise since coming out of "retirement." (In May that year he recorded his *Some Nice Things I've Missed* LP.)

Ol' Blue Eyes Is Back! understated it. Recordings, television specials, film appearances, nightclub performances, U.S. and overseas concert tours, and his fans were happy again.

Ol' Blue Eyes Is Back on November 17, 1973 *TV Guide* cover.

Price tag for Magnavox specials.

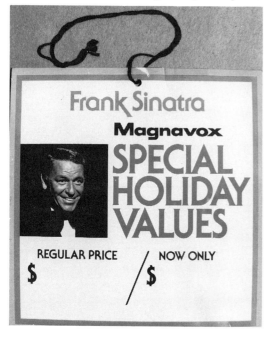

Frank Sinatra

Magnavox

SPECIAL HOLIDAY VALUES

REGULAR PRICE / NOW ONLY

$ / $

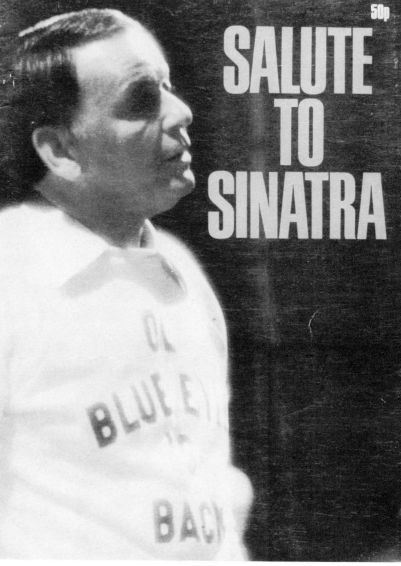

50p

SALUTE TO SINATRA

Sunday, Nov. 18th · 8:30 PM · Channel ② ⑧ ⑫

Magnavox presents Frank Sinatra

Simulated TV picture.

The television event of the season: Ol' Blue Eyes is Back!

with Special Guest Star Gene Kelly

Be sure to watch this truly *special* Special. And visit your participating Magnavox dealer now for a wide selection of color TVs, stereo consoles and other Holiday Special Values, like these:

6-PIECE STEREO COMPONENT SYSTEM

- AM/FM stereo radio.
- Record and 8-track tape players.
- Two speakers.
- Stereo headphones.
- Mobile cart.

PLUS 2 free LP records. Complete, only $159.95.

SAVE $40!

EXCLUSIVE RECORD OFFER!

Available at Magnavox dealers, custom Reprise recording starring The Association, Count Basie, Harpers Bizarre, Don Ho, Barbara McNair, Nelson Riddle and Frank Sinatra!

ONLY **$1.25**

$2.50 for 8-track tape.

All prices minimum Fair Trade. Optional with dealers in non-Fair Trade states.

Produced by Howard W. Koch   Directed by Marty Pasetta   Written by Fred Ebb   Executive Producer Alfred di Scipio

Tribute magazine from England.

192

Medallion for Sinatra's triumphant return to Vegas as "The Noblest Roman of Them All," residing at Caesars Palace.

Menu from Caesars is red velour with gold print.

Ashtray from Caesars Palace.

72. Television 1973–1990

Less than a year after *Ol' Blue Eyes Is Back!* aired on NBC, Frank appeared "live" from New York City's Madison Square Garden, on the ABC special, *The Main Event*. The show was treated like a sporting event and produced by ABC's team from "Monday Night Football" coverage, including commentary from Howard Cosell. Another ABC special, *Sinatra and Friends*, aired April 21, 1977.

Sinatra's fortieth anniversary in show business (starting with the Harry James experience) became the theme of Sinatra's sixty-fourth birthday bash at Caesars Palace, taped by NBC. Celebrities paid tribute to Frank and the show con-

cluded with a Sinatra mini-concert, and aired January 3, 1980.

Ten years later, Sinatra came full circle, return-

The Main Event is televised "live" on ABC, October 13, 1974, and then released on record by Reprise. Here are the promotional poster and standee.

194

ing to CBS for a TV special in honor of his seventy-fifth Birthday. Taped on his birthday at the Meadowlands Arena in New Jersey, the special aired four days later. Historic footage intercut with current concert material allowed the nation to share in Sinatra's Diamond Jubilee. From his TV debut in 1950 through the 1990 birthday special, the first forty years of Sinatra on TV have provided hundreds of hours of great entertainment. Video tape will keep these shows alive for generations to come.

ABC airs *Sinatra and Friends* April 21, 1977, and Sinatra again appears on *TV Guide* cover.

The Man and His Music, a Sinatra one-man show on NBC, November 22, 1981.

Sinatra appears on NBC: top left, *Laugh-In*, November 2, 1977, with Lenny Schultz; top right, *The Tonight Show*, November 12, 1976, with Johnny Carson, lower left, *Contract on Cherry Street* airs November 19, 1977; lower right, *Dean Martin Celebrity Roast* for Frank on February 7, 1978.

Sinatra celebrates forty years of show business with a special from Caesars Palace, televised January 3, 1980.

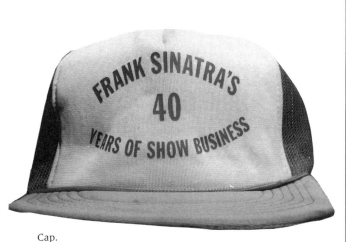

Cap.

Invitation to fortieth anniversary is attractive plaque.

Guests at fortieth anniversary receive music box that plays "My Way."

Frank Sinatra Celebrates His 40th Anniversary

Magazine from Caesars Palace honors Frank's fortieth.

TV GUIDE

Feb. 3-9
75¢

OH, WHAT A WEEK!

February is off with a bang

This week on TV (clockwise from top): Lesley Ann Warren of 'Family of Spies'; the *Amen* wedding; Jennifer Grey of 'Murder in Mississippi'; and Sammy Davis Jr. with friends in tribute to his career.

ABC airs tribute to Sammy Davis, Jr., on February 4, 1990.

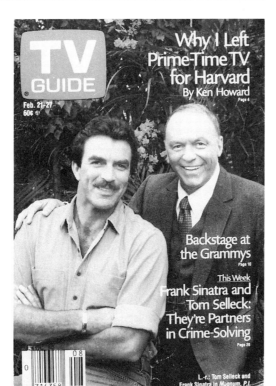

TV GUIDE

Why I Left Prime-Time TV for Harvard
By Ken Howard
Page 4

Feb. 21-27
60¢

Backstage at the Grammys
Page 10

This Week
Frank Sinatra and Tom Selleck: They're Partners in Crime-Solving
Page 26

L.-r.: Tom Selleck and Frank Sinatra in *Magnum, P.I.*

Sinatra appears with Tom Selleck on *Magnum, P.I.* episode on CBS, February 25, 1987.

199

73. Reprise Records (1973–1990)

French 45 rpm single.

Counter display from Holland.

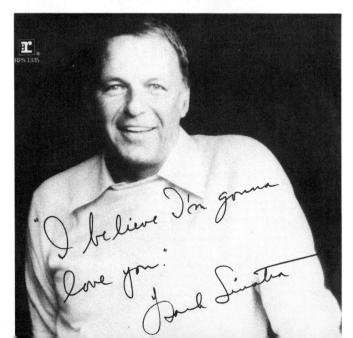

Sticker from England promoting *Portrait of Sinatra* LP.

Plastic cut-out to
promote 1980 *Trilogy* release.

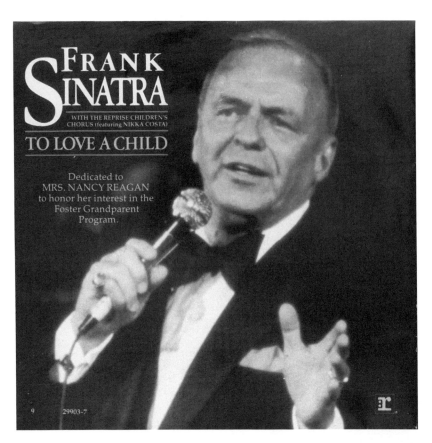

Issued in 1982, honoring Nancy
Reagan's Foster Grandparent
program.

Frank Sinatra

A Baby Just Like You B/W Christmas Mem'ries

Produced and Arranged by Don Costa

RPS 1342 ©1975 Warner Bros. Records Inc./Made in U.S.A.

Grampa Frank's little Angela
Jennifer on this 1975 single.

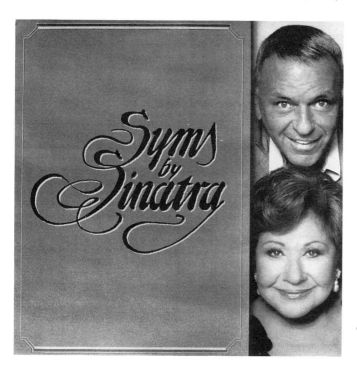

Sinatra conducts for Sylvia Syms
on this 1982 LP.

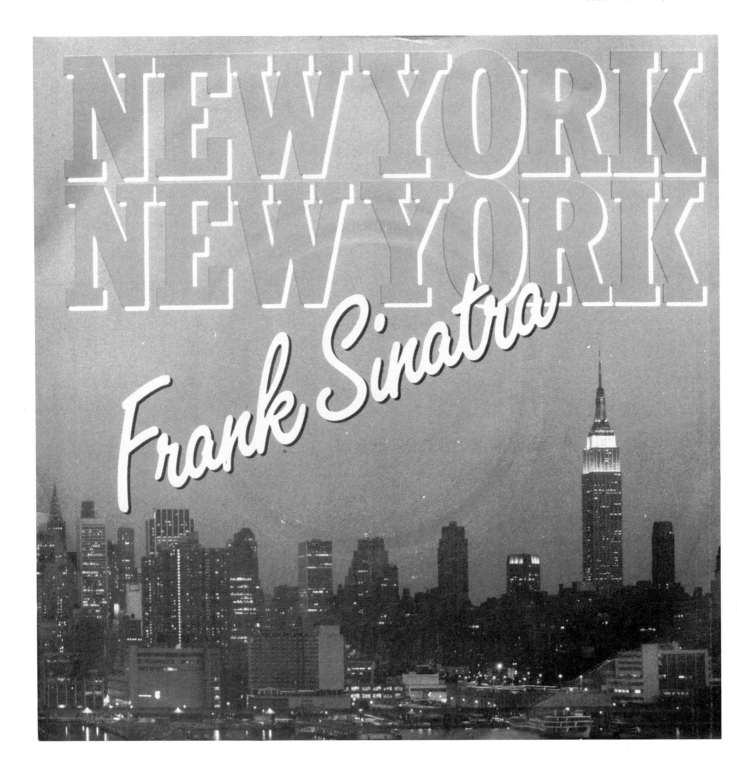

to "L.A. Is My Lady."

The Reprise Collection issued 1990 for Sinatra's seventy-fifth Birthday.

Collectors with jukeboxes seek the original title strips.

France.

Belgium.

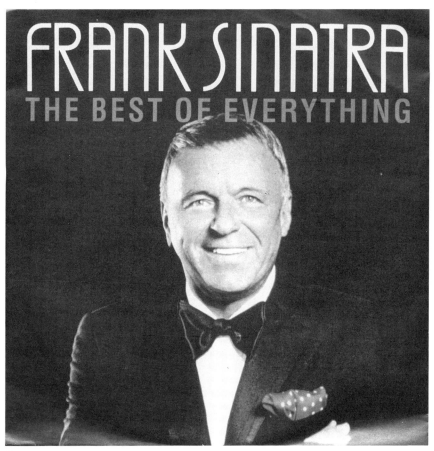

Germany.

Holland.

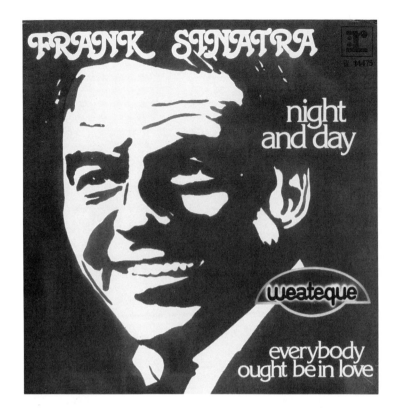

Italy.

Portugal.

Japan.

208

LPs from Brazil released 1979 to celebrate "40 Years of Records" from Sinatra.

England.

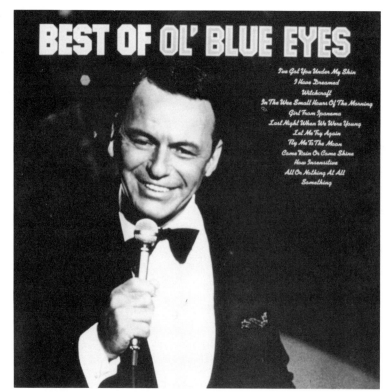

France.

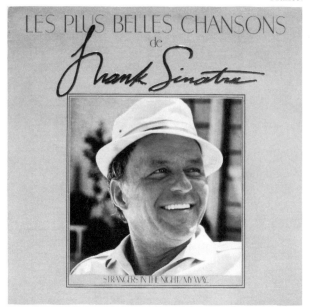

Japan.

210

74. That's Entertainment!

(1974)

and

That's Entertainment, Part 2

(1976)

One-sheet.

Lobby cards.

75. **Contract on Cherry Street**

(1977)

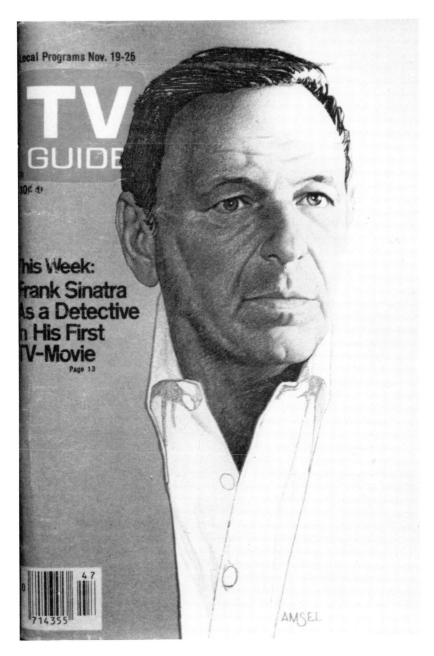

CONTRACT ON CHERRY STREET

Frank Sinatra's TV-movie debut, a 1977 story about cops and mobsters.

Sinatra is Deputy Inspector Frank Hovannes, a 25-year veteran of the New York Police Department who heads a unit that fights organized crime. At least it tries to. Lately, departmental regulations have been getting in the way, and when a fellow officer is murdered, Hovannes decides that he's had enough. He and three other unit members break the rules by ambushing—and killing—an underworld chieftain. The plan to turn two rival mobs against each other.

Filmed in New York City.

Supporting Cast . . . Weinberg: Martin Balsam. Emily: Verna Bloom. Polito: Harry Guardino. Obregon: Henry Silva. Savage: Michael Nouri. Waldman: Martin Gabel. Eddie Manzaro: Marco St. John. Palmini: James Luisi. Kittens: Richard Ward. Seruto: Joe de Santis. Tommy Sinardos: Jay Black. Bob Halloran: Addison Powell. Fran Marks: Steve Inwood. Otis Washington: Johnny Barnes. Phil Lombardi: Lenny Montana. Richie Saint: Murray Moston. (Repeat; 3 hrs.)

Frank Sinatra

Frank Sinatra (right) and Henry Silva portray two New York City police detectives who become angered when one of their comrades is slain -- and set out to attack the mob in their own way -- in "Contract on Cherry Street," on NBC-TV's "The Big Event," Tuesday, August 1.

76. **The First Deadly Sin**

(1980)

Movie edition pocketbook
from England.

Belgian poster.

HBO guide.

German movie program.

77. **Cannonball Run II**

(1 9 8 4)

Sheet music.

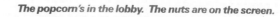

One-sheet poster.

78. Listen Up: The Lives of Quincy Jones

(1990)

Sinatra and musician, arranger, composer, and producer Quincy Jones run through an arrangement during a moment from Warner Bros.'
Listen Up: The Lives Of Quincy Jones.

LADIES' HOME JOURNAL

SEPTEMBER 1974/60¢

Journal

JOAN KENNEDY
Woman under pressure

INFLATION FIGHTERS
Cost-cutting secrets of
American families

**HOW TO CHANGE YOUR
LOOKS — AND OUTLOOK**
8-page beauty bonus

PSYCHIC
How Edgar Cayce
"saved" his dying wife

DECORATING
What's pretty — and what isn't

**JAMES A. MICHENER'S
"CENTENNIAL"**
Stirring excerpt from
the novel of the year

HORMONE THERAPY
Can it give you extra
years of vitality?

HOME REPAIRS
A Ralph Nader exposé

*Love Song
To My First
Granddaughter
By FRANK
SINATRA
plus exclusive first photos*

The New York Times Magazine

**OUTLASTING
ROCK**
Sophisticated
Melody
And Lyrics
Make a
Comeback
By Sidney Zion

YOUR FALL & WINTER ARTS AND ENTERTAINMENT GUIDE ■ SEXY CARS
ARE BACK! ■ THE QUAKERS VS. THE JEWS ■ BEST ALLERGY MEDICINE

Philadelphia

SEPTEMBER 1983 $1.95

**THE
SELLING
OF
SINATRA
& THE PLAN TO
CONQUER THE
BOARDWALK!**

PLUS
INSIDE
PHILADELPHIA'S
COLLEGES:
A SPECIAL REPORT

Gran Milán

*è in
edicola*

GranMilán
benvenuto FRANK
la cultura chiama
Milano risponde

**PER
CONOSCERE
TUTTO QUANTO AVVIENE
NELLA VERA CAPITALE D'ITALIA**

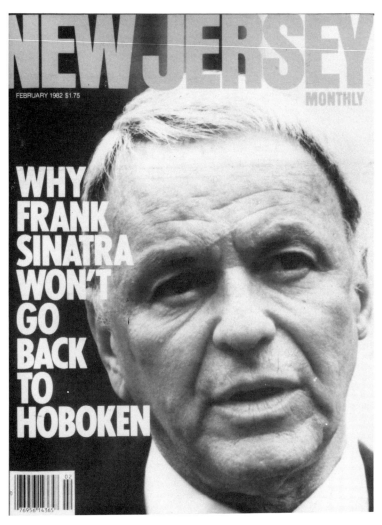

NEW JERSEY MONTHLY

FEBRUARY 1982 $1.75

WHY FRANK SINATRA WON'T GO BACK TO HOBOKEN

The Spectator
HAMILTON, AUGUST 16 TO AUGUST 23, 198

TV TIMES

Frank Sinatra :
A kindly
64-year-old
Grandfather

THE ORDEAL OF OUR HOSTAGE HEROES

An insider's poignant story of the fight to free them and a look at their challenge now: making new lives

People weekly

FRANK SINATRA

inaugurates a cleaned-up act

Anthony Hopkins is as hot as his tub scene with Bo Derek

Nancy Reagan's cosmetics guru

221

Supplemento al n. 40 di GENTE del 3/10/86
Spedizione in abbonamento postale gruppo II/70

GENTE

sinatra

RUSCONI EDITORE • L. 3000

LA SUA LEGGENDA
Numero speciale di 124 pagine
dedicato alla voce più bella del mondo

CHIPS

AUGUST, 1981

$2.95

FOR THE WINNERS OF THE WORLD

SINATRA
WINNER TAKE ALL

KEN USTON
CARD-COUNTING WIZARD

BASEBALL FEVER
WHO'S ON FIRST?

SHOWTIME
'BOARDWALK MAGIC'

ADDED ACTION
THE DEALER'S DILEMMA
RENO/TAHOE UPDATE
HORSES & 'BODY LANGUAGE'
PROFILE: MARLENE RICCI
GAMBLING COLLECTIBLES
RODEO DRIVE: BRASSY CLASS
RACING THE THUNDERBOATS
THE SYSTEMS GAMBIT
GUIDE TO GAMESMANSHIP

Chicago Tribune · SUNDAY, AUGUST 26, 1986 ● SECTION 13

BOOKS
Stephen King: Mr. Horror

The ARTS

SINATRA TALKS
For 50 years he has sung America's songs.
Now he reveals what they mean to him.

| Miles Davis heads a lively Jazz Fest | Chuck Norris gets serious | Rethinking the art in our public places |

80. Sheet Music of the 1970s

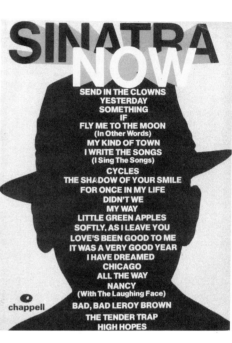

81. International LPs

Brazil.

Apple shaped picture disc
from England.

Picture disc from Germany.

LA VOCE

UN MITO

VOL. 2

Italy.

FRANK SINATRA
INIMITABILE

Variety
REL-ST 19185
STEREO

LITTLE WHITE LIES - PISTOL PACKIM'MAMA - SPEAK LOW - MY IDEAL - WOODY WOOD PECKER SONG -
ALMOST LIKE BOING IN LOVE - JINGLE BELLS - YOU DO - TREE IN THE MEADOW - LOVE SOMEBODY -
HOW SOON - SERENADE OF THE BELLS

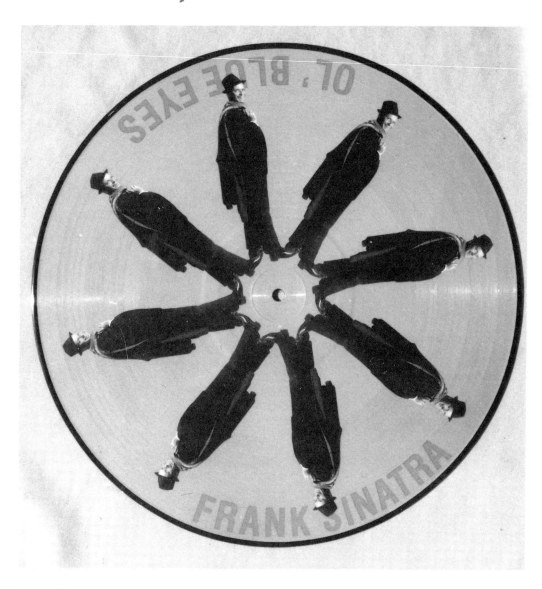

Picture discs from The Netherlands.

Picture disc from The Netherlands.

Spain.

This poster was displayed in schools.
Frankie was an early force for tolerance.

This 1940s bracelet is worth a bit more
than the original one dollar cost.

Sinatra for Garrard turntables, early 1960s.

Sinatra became spokesman for an ailing Chrysler Corporation in 1980. A limited edition, blue as Sinatra's eyes, named the Imperial FS was a tempting collectible. I settled for this Chrysler showroom pamphlet.

Sinatra in 1990 advertising campaign for All Nippon Airways.

83. The Books

Published in 1976 and used in elementary schools.

The first book on Sinatra, 1946.

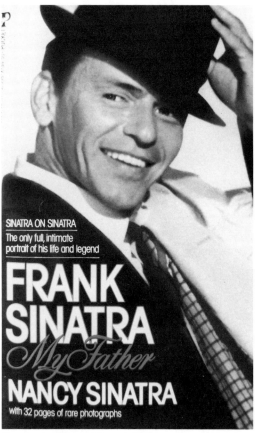

Paperback edition of Nancy's book.

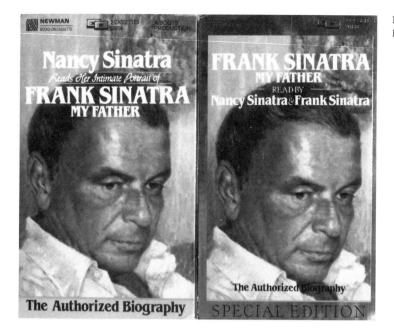

Left, Nancy reads her book on cassettes. Right, Frank and Nancy read on the special edition.

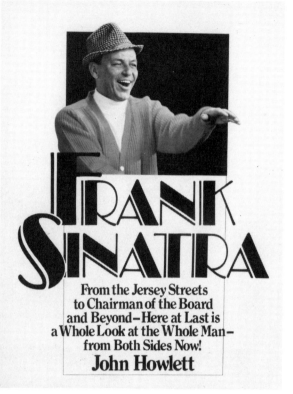

SINATRA

THE GERMAN WAY

by
KONSTANTIN SHADOW

SVERIGE

FRANK SINATRA

1953

inkl. KÖPENHAMN

av Börje Fredriksson

JACQUES HARVEY

MONSIEUR SINATRA

AM ALBIN MICHEL

Songs by SINATRA 1973-1976

The SINATRA Directory A-Z 1939-1976

A Discography of Alternate Takes

Brian Hainsworth

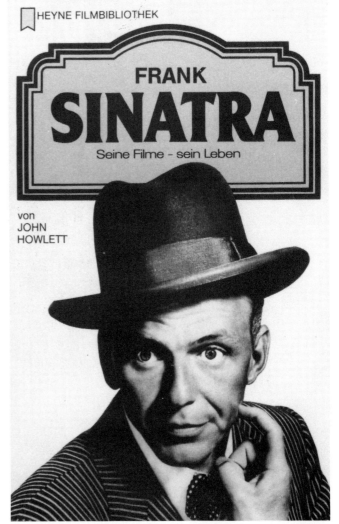

HEYNE FILMBIBLIOTHEK

FRANK SINATRA

Seine Filme – sein Leben

von JOHN HOWLETT

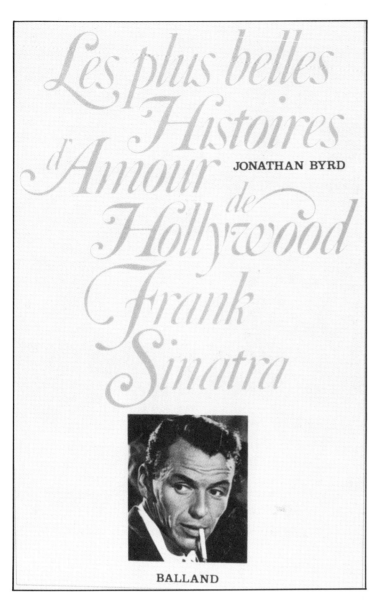

Les plus belles Histoires d'Amour de Hollywood

JONATHAN BYRD

Frank Sinatra

BALLAND

THE FILMS OF
FRANK SINATRA

By G. Ringgold, C. McCarty

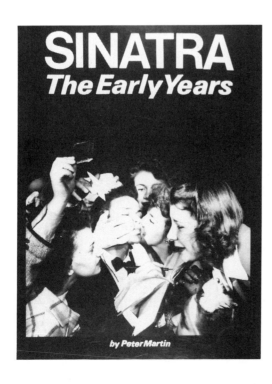

SINATRA
The Early Years

by Peter Martin

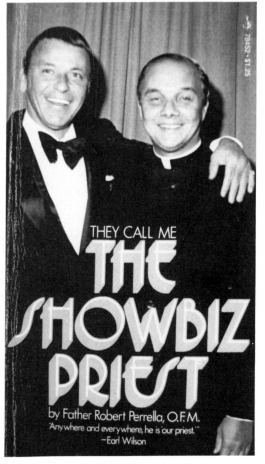

THEY CALL ME
THE SHOWBIZ PRIEST

by Father Robert Perrella, O.F.M.
"Anywhere and everywhere, he is our priest."
—Earl Wilson

FRANK SINATRA
The Man, The Myth and The Music
by Peter Goddard

70-165 $1.25

The fascinating story of one of the most incredible entertainers the world has ever known

SINATRA

AN AMERICAN CLASSIC

JOHN ROCKWELL

FRANK SINATRA
OL' BLUE EYES

A CANDID PORTRAIT OF AMERICA'S GREATEST ENTERTAINER
BY NORM GOLDSTEIN AND THE ASSOCIATED PRESS

236

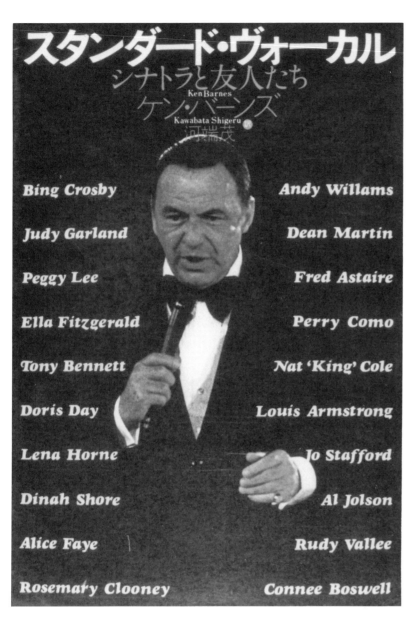

スタンダード・ヴォーカル
シナトラと友人たち
Ken Barnes
ケン・バーンズ
Kawabata Shigeru
河端茂

Bing Crosby	Andy Willams
Judy Garland	Dean Martin
Peggy Lee	Fred Astaire
Ella Fitzgerald	Perry Como
Tony Bennett	Nat 'King' Cole
Doris Day	Louis Armstrong
Lena Horne	Jo Stafford
Dinah Shore	Al Jolson
Alice Faye	Rudy Vallee
Rosemary Clooney	Connee Boswell

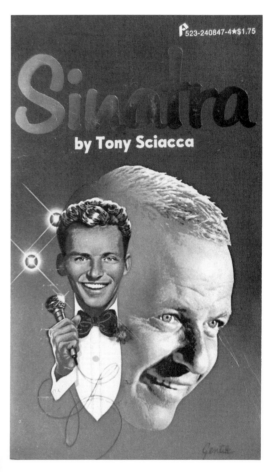

523-240847-4 ★ $1.75

Sinatra

by Tony Sciacca

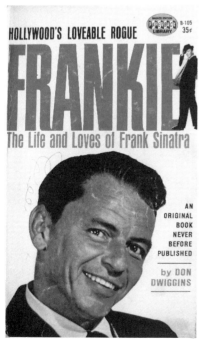

HOLLYWOOD'S LOVEABLE ROGUE

PAPERBACK LIBRARY B-105 35¢

FRANKIE

The Life and Loves of Frank Sinatra

AN ORIGINAL BOOK NEVER BEFORE PUBLISHED

by DON DWIGGINS

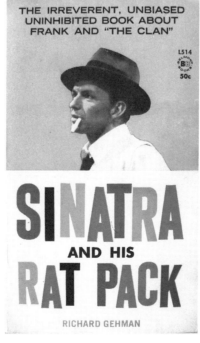

THE IRREVERENT, UNBIASED UNINHIBITED BOOK ABOUT FRANK AND "THE CLAN"

L514
BELMONT BOOKS
50c

SINATRA

AND HIS

RAT PACK

RICHARD GEHMAN

237

84. The Concerts and Programs

The concerts and club dates are too numerous to detail. However, I have heard of one collector who keeps a daily diary on Frank's activities. There's most likely an audience-made cassette tape of every concert given by Sinatra after his "retirement" months. Portable recorders are conveniently concealed yet provide a remarkable audio reproduction. The more serious audio collector wants tapes of every concert and documents the songs performed on each date.

Some collectors "specialize" in concert programs, which vary from a single page bearing Sinatra's name to the elaborate book-size programs sold at various venues.

Is the total number of photos taken of Sinatra a conceivable figure? The bobby-soxers of the forties swapped photos among the various Sinatra fan clubs that existed. Many of those bobby-soxers continue to follow Frank and to photograph him at every opportunity. Certainly no one can have *all* the photos.

Program from Verona, Italy, June 20, 1987.

Concert ticket, Tokyo, April 17, 1985.

Poster promoting Sinatra in Tokyo, April 17–19, 1985.

Frank, Dean and Sammy
"Together Again" tour, March
1988.

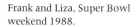

(souvenir buttons)

Frank and Liza, Super Bowl
weekend 1988.

Others collect memories — images of past concerts and club appearances. The kid, the Voice, the Swinger, the Chairman, the consummate performer, Ol' Blue Eyes, the Old Man (affectionately). Song titles, bits of lyrics, a few notes strung together that we can hum. He fills our recollections with the good things of which memories are made.

Poster for "The Ultimate Event" in Tokyo, February 25, 1989.

Liza replaces Dean for "The Ultimate Event" 1988. Life-size standee.

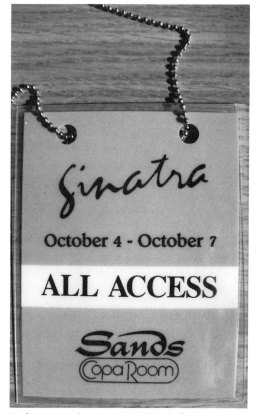

Backstage pass for Sinatra's 1990 "Back at the Sands."

Plastic facsimiles of Sinatra's Brunswick record, hung from the ceiling at Harrah's, Tahoe, to celebrate the disc's fiftieth anniversary.

(souvenir shirt)

Program from second annual Sinatra Celebrity Invitational Golf Tournament, February 1990.

Program from Kleinhans Music Hall, Buffalo, New York, April 1951.

Travel poster. Sinatra and Vegas are synonymous.

Resorts International is the first Casino to open in Atlantic City, and Sinatra is there in April 1979. Commemorative matches.

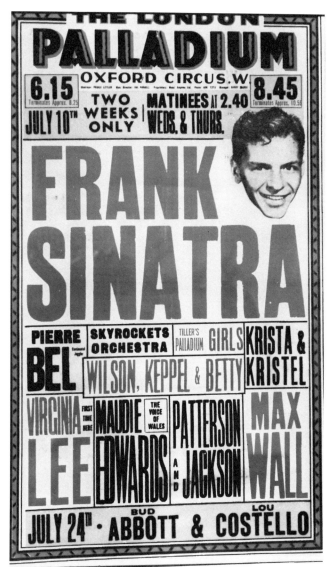

Poster for an early 1950s appearance at London's Palladium.

Music for the Wounded 1947 fund-raiser includes Danny Kaye, Al Jolson, Jimmy Durante, Red Skelton, Phil Silvers, and Sinatra.

Program from Maracana stadium, Brazil, January 26, 1980. Attendance at this soccer stadium set a *Guinness Book* record for a single concert.

The program for the 1984 Royal Albert Hall shows was record-shaped.

When fighter Ray Mancini injured a collarbone, this May 1983 event scheduled for Sun City, South Africa, was canceled.

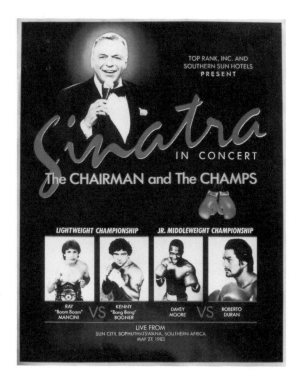

Program for London's Royal Festival Hall and Royal Albert Hall concerts, September 1980.

Program from May-June 1975 European tour.

A 1982 Radio City Music Hall benefit for Sloan-Kettering Cancer Center.

Poster advertises Sinatra at Carnegie Hall, September 1981.

85. Postcards

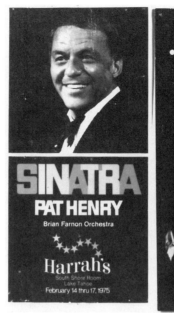

Sinatra

FRANK + NANCY

MUSICAL CONDUCTOR, JOE PARNELLO
BRIAN FARNON ORCHESTRA
Thru March 14, 1983

Harrah's
Lake Tahoe

Sinatra

Pat Henry
The Little Steps

Brian Farnon Orchestra
January 23, 24 & 25, 1976

Harrah's
South Shore Room • Lake Tahoe

Frank Sinatra

Bill Miller, Conducting
Jackie Gayle
Brian Farnon Orchestra
Thru October 27, 1977

Harrah's
South Shore Room, Lake Tahoe

FRANK SINATRA
BILL MILLER CONDUCTING

PAT HENRY

Harrah's
SOUTH SHORE ROOM
LAKE TAHOE

BRIAN FARNON ORCHESTRA
THRU MARCH 31, 1977

HOME OF FRANK SINATRA, BEVERLY HILLS, CALIFORNIA

John
Denver
Performs For The
Dinner Show Only

Frank
Sinatra
Pat Henry
Play The Cocktail Show

Brian Farnon Orchestra
AUGUST 1 thru 7, 1975

Harrah's
SOUTH SHORE ROOM • LAKE TAHOE

FRANK SINATRA
THE MAN AND HIS MUSIC
NOVEMBER
2-5

FRANK SINATRA
THE MAN AND HIS MUSIC
SEPTEMBER
14-17

86. Home Video

MGM/UA

MGM/UA

MGM/UA

Packaging on this British video is different than the
U.S.

RCA/Columbia

RCA/Columbia

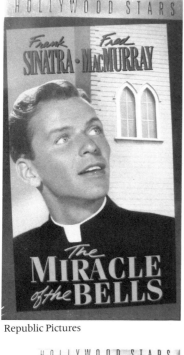

Republic Pictures

RCA/Columbia

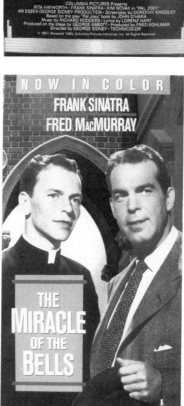

Republic Pictures

Republic Pictures

Warner

Turner

Turner

Warner

Warner

Turner

Warner   Warner

Colorized version of *Suddenly*.

First of the home videos. Distributed through Magnetic Video.

Kodak released *The Ultimate Event* in 1989.

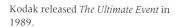

Video from Avon cosmetics.

April 1985 Tokyo concert on laser disc from Japan.

MCA.

A Man And His Music (1965), *Sinatra + Ella + Jobim* (1967), and *Ol' Blue Eyes Is Back* (1973) comprise *The Reprise Collection* issued for Sinatra's seventy-fifth birthday in 1990.

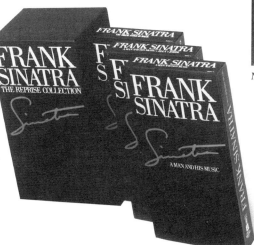

251

87. **Fan Clubs**

A variety of Frank Sinatra fan clubs have existed since the early 1940s. Today there are clubs in Australia, Belgium, England, Holland, Japan, and Sweden, to name just a few. The author has been involved with the International Sinatra Society since 1974, and is currently the club's president. The club's magazine offers all the latest Sinatra news and product with publications every two months. For more information write: International Sinatra Society, P.O. Box 5195, Anderson, South Carolina, 29623.

Fourth anniversary issue of *Swoon Time News,* 1948 fan club publication.

Recent issues from the International Sinatra Society. New members are welcome.

Sinatra Society membership card.

252

88. **Some Nice Things I've Missed**

There are collectible items associated with Sinatra's career which cannot be categorized. Like the title of his 1974 Reprise album, here are "Some Nice Things I've Missed."

Binoculars offered at Frank's concert at Palatrussardi, Milan, Italy, September 27, 1986.

Souvenir pillow of Frank, Liza and Sammy's "Ultimate Event" performance in Amsterdam, April 27, 1989.

It's always Sinatra time with this clock.

A napkin from Sinatra's private jet.

Tag on key ring reads "Love & Peace Frank Sinatra."

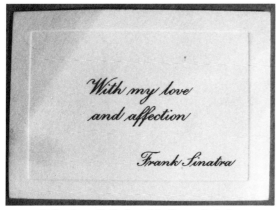

With my love
and affection

Frank Sinatra

Personal "thank you" gifts from Mr. Sinatra include:

Personalized cigarette lighter.

The famous handkerchiefs he gives away come in red and orange.

A deck of diamond queens was promotional item for the MGM/UA Home Video release of *The Manchurian Candidate*.

Young At Heart commemorative plate issued 1987.

Napkin and ashtray from Jilly's in New York City, one of Sinatra's favorite Big Apple hangouts in the 1960s and 1970s.

Hat sold during concert tour.

This napkin states Sinatra's philosophy.

Bronze medallion.

Medallion commemorates opening of Cleveland's Coliseum Oct. 26, 1976.

254

Sinatra introduced his sauces in 1990. These are collectibles that taste good too.